✓ II 5/86 - 9/86

-8-80

12-61 → 5/92

D0907088

HOG WILD

HOG WILD

THE AUTOBIOGRAPHY OF FRANK BROYLES

by Frank Broyles with Jim Bailey

MEMPHIS

Memphis State University Press

FOR BARBARA

CONTENTS

PREFACE

When the people at Memphis State University Press first spoke to me about doing a book, I felt both flattered and apprehensive. It's a heady thing to know a publisher wants your life and career between hard covers, but at the same time I feared they had contacted the wrong man.

"Don't you want somebody controversial?", I asked. "Somebody like Woody Hayes?"

"Frank, you're more controversial than you think," one of them said. "Remember the pooch kick? Remember. . . ."

For some reason, I did not care to pursue that angle. "Well, at least you'd want somebody funny and colorful," I said, struggling to create a diversion. "Lou Holtz can pop one-liners for hours. John McKay has great wit. Darrell Royal has such a vivid, folksy way of expressing himself, he's added whole phrases to the language. I never said anything like 'we're gonna dance with who brung us'."

"Don't sell yourself short, Frank. You created a new word right there on national television. Audiblize. No English teacher could find it anywhere."

"You need somebody with great charisma," I persisted. "Nobody has charisma like Bear Bryant."

"Bear's done his book, Frank. They all have. All except you."

"But, every game the Razorbacks play is hashed and rehashed

5000 times in Arkansas," I said. "What could I tell Arkansas fans that they don't know? They remember everything."

"You'd be surprised, Frank. Nobody remembers anything any more. The other day on Hollywood Squares, nobody knew what year man first set foot on the moon."

"Why, I know that," I said. "That happened the year we installed AstroTurf at Fayetteville for Big Shootout I. You see, Texas and Arkansas were one and two in the nation, and ABC talked us into moving the game to December, and the President came, and. . . ."

"Uh, just put it on paper, Frank."

Not really. The preceding dialogue, I have to confess, is highly exaggerated. I promise you the rest of this project will be as candid and accurate as memory and research enable me to make it. I had misgivings, but it took me about two seconds to resolve them. A man who spent his life with some of the greatest coaches and athletes in the world cannot reject a chance to try to explain them.

Every book needs a dedication, and this one could appropriately go to all the people of Arkansas, to all my former players, to my family, to any number of special friends. Still, this is an easier decision than any I ever made on the field. This book is for Barbara.

Frank Broyles

Fayetteville, Ark.
June 15, 1979

1
COACHING'S ANCIENT DREAM

Quite inadvertently, Bobby Dodd whetted my interest in the University of Arkansas years ago when I was an assistant coach at Georgia Tech. We'd be sitting around in a staff meeting, griping about some recruiting tug-of-war we were having with the University of Georgia Bulldogs. Dodd would say, "Boys, just think what we could do if there was no Georgia—only a Georgia Tech." The one-state, one-team concept is, I suppose, an ancient dream of coaching. I already knew of such a place. I'd seen it while working for Bob Woodruff at Baylor University.

Arkansas!

In 1949, it was obvious Woodruff would soon move from Baylor. About the same time, John Barnhill left the field at Arkansas because of his health. Barnie offered Woodruff the job as Arkansas head coach, and I remember standing in Woodruff's office and urging, "Bob, take it, take it, take it. And take me with you." I'd seen Arkansas athletes like Clyde Scott, Muscles Campbell, Billy Hix, Fred Williams and Dave Hanner. I'd sensed the statewide commitment. Woodruff and I went to Florida instead, but I was wild about the Arkansas job every time it came open.

During four years as a college player (Tech) and 30 as an assistant coach (Baylor, Florida, Tech) and head coach (Missouri, Arkansas), I was associated with teams that won 266 games and visited 21 bowls. During my 19 years as head coach of the University of Arkansas, our teams won 144, lost 58, and tied five, won or shared seven Southwest Conference championships, won a national title in the midst of a 22-game winning streak, and made 10 bowl trips.

Those are figures you can find in the library, and I pledge I'll avoid statistical overkill, but I think I should set the record down here so it'll be clear what my friends refer to when they ask, as they occasionally still do, "Don't you miss coaching, Frank? Be honest."

No, I don't. I loved coaching as much as any man fortunate enough to get a coaching job, but I was much more fortunate than most. I landed the only job I every really wanted, at Arkansas, and I was permitted to leave coaching at the time of my choosing, in the manner of my choosing, and I was permitted to designate my successor. You'd be astonished how few men in the profession have been so totally blessed in those four categories.

I thought 30 years was long enough to be on the field, and 20 years was enough to make peace with the unique pressures that go with a head-coaching position in major college football. Goodness knows, I'm not knocking those who stay longer or get out sooner. I quit when I thought the time was right for me, and I haven't had one second's regret.

How could I? I've been too busy the last two years, running around to the Orange Bowl and the Fiesta Bowl, the NCAA basketball tournament, the College World Series, calling the hogs for Lou Holtz's Razorbacks, Eddie Sutton's Razorbacks, and Norm De-Briyn's Razorbacks as our total program exploded into levels we only dreamed about a few years ago. No, I'm not an embittered ex-football coach. I'm the happiest athletic director in the United States. If things were any better for me, I couldn't stand it.

What makes John Franklin Broyles tick? It's easy to assess others—we do it every day in ordinary conversation—but how does a man explain himself? A detached viewpoint is out of the question.

Looking for help, I scanned many things written about me over the years. I read that, as a young coach, I was brash, impatient, rabid, enthusiastic, frantic. That merely confirms what I already knew. I found a lot of humorous references to my Georgia accent (all coming after I left Georgia, of course) and to the fact I had a lot of trouble keeping my shirt-tail tucked in while I fretted up and down the sideline. Who wants to be remembered as the coach with the flapping shirt-tail?

I read that I was a "super salesman" always receptive to new ideas and trends. Too receptive in some cases. The first thing I did after I came to Arkansas was to sell myself on an offensive system that turned out to be a galloping disaster. Each summer I discover a new grip, swing, or stance that I am certain will revolutionize the game of golf. Lon Ferrell, who has been with me as a coach and administrator nearly two decades, says I'm the most optimistic person he's ever known. "He's such an optimist," Lon says, "that if he were being run out of town, he'd think he was leading a parade." A good line, but I believe I could detect the difference.

I've heard that I was "too soft" because I sometimes gave football players second, third, and even fourth chances to stay in school, stay with the program. If that's a fault, I'll cheerfully plead guilty. For every time I was taken advantage of, I could see a dozen other youngsters settle down and re-direct their lives in ways that promised something for them after they left football.

I found many speculative stories linking me with other jobs, especially in my first few years with the Razorbacks. Truthfully, I would have left Arkansas only at the head of one of Lon's "parades".

I maintain a person should look forward, never backward. When it comes to the Razorbacks, though, Arkansas people love to do both. I'm no exception. I still see Lance Alworth running SMU ragged in 1959, I still see Mickey Cissell's field goal fluttering toward the cross bar at Austin in '60, and I still see Jerry Lamb or Bobby Crockett or Chuck Dicus making the impossible catch. I still hear the extra loud thump that meant the tackle was by Wayne Harris or Loyd Phillips or Ronnie Caveness. I remember the great character of a lot of youngsters who were not great football players physically, but who played with a fanatical determination to win for Arkansas. I remember the tremendous things, and I also remember the disappointments and frustrations and near-misses.

Indulge me. Could we go over it again, just one more time?

2
A KID FOR ALL SEASONS

From the time I was six years old, as long as I can remember, I wanted to be an athlete and only that. I grew up going to school, playing ball in the afternoon—whatever sport was in season—and coming home. My mother would always have my dinner in the oven; the family had already eaten. I'd eat, read the sports pages of the Atlanta *Constitution* and *Journal,* and go to bed about 7:30. The next day, I'd get up, go to school, play ball, come home, eat, read the sports pages, and go to bed—the same unvarying pattern for years and years, all through my childhood.

I did hold a job for two weeks when I was about 16 years old, and that's the only job other than playing or coaching or administering athletics that I've ever had in my life. Even that two-week job was, in a way, sports-oriented. I played semi-pro baseball for the Dixie Steel team, and Dixie Steel put me to work bluing nails. That's the finishing process, and it is very tough and tedious work over a hot furnace. You'd "blue" those nails in the furnace and keg them up, and somebody would haul them off. All day long. I was making $18 a week for bluing nails and playing ball, but then the American Legion group came to see my daddy.

"Hey," they said. "Frank's got to play for the Legion team." My daddy was in business selling cars, and the Legion boosters included some of his best customers. Daddy and I agreed it was best that I leave Dixie Steel and go back to Legion ball. I can't say that I missed the nails.

Most of the time I was growing up, I planned to be a major league baseball player. When I was eight years old, I could tell you the starting line-ups and batting averages of the 16 major-league teams. When they shifted line-ups and moved somebody out of the clean-up spot, I knew about it. Every Sunday afternoon I was at the news-stand waiting for the new copy of *The Sporting News* to be delivered. I devoured it from cover to cover. That went on until I was nearly 30 years old and working as an assistant football coach at Georgia Tech.

Atlanta has encircled it now, but Decatur was a suburban bed-room community in my youth. Most of the people worked in Atlanta. Decatur had no business or industry of its own except grocery stores and the like. You passed through it on the way to Stone Mountain and Athens. Decatur did have a lot of vacant lots, and that was important to me. I kicked footballs on vacant lots. I played baseball on vacant lots. You always had a place to practice and play.

Most of the members of my family were big sports fans. Compared to anybody else, that is. Compared to me, they had only a moderate interest in athletics. The Broyles family had been in Georgia a long time. They were railroad people. My grandfather, R. A. Broyles, was a top administrator with the Georgia railroad and, about the turn of the century, he started a grocery business on the side. Eventually he worked up to about 25 stores in the Atlanta area. My father, O. T. Broyles, worked in the Broyles Grocery Stores from the time he was 11 years old. I'm not sure if he graduated from high school.

I do remember very vividly an impression he made on me when I was 12 or 13. He caught me smoking a cigarette. I can't recall if it was real tobacco or cornsilks, but he really laid down the law. "Look," he said. "When I was your age, I was helping my parents put food on the table. You're not working; you're playing games. Well, smoking and games don't mix. You can stop smoking and keep on playing, or you can go to work." I knew a bargain when I heard one. I never smoked again.

When my grandfather retired, he gave three grocery stores to each of the three sons who had been in business with him. My father lost his three stores because he was just too good-hearted to collect during the Depression. He was in and out of the grocery business several times, but credit always finished him. He just couldn't bring himself to do the things you had to do to collect. I remember delivering produce for him on my bike when I was about 10 years old because we didn't have enough money to put gas in the car.

My dad eventually operated a successful insurance agency, but he went directly from the grocery stores to the car business. He sold cars with the Chevrolet agency at Decatur, and we had a new car, a demonstrator, all the time through the late 1930s. Things were picking up for us as I was coming of age. Otherwise, I might have had to put aside athletics and go to work as my older brothers did.

My mother's maiden name was Solms. Her mother and father came over from Germany and married here. My mother couldn't speak English when she enrolled for the first grade. They wouldn't let her in; she had to take a crash tutoring course in English before she started to school.

My maternal grandmother was the most strong-willed person I ever knew, and my mother is the next most strong-willed person. Barbara says I'm a spittin' image of my mother. My size, for sure, came from my mother. She was 5-9 and big-boned. All her brothers were big; she came from an athletic family. My father was only 5-7, and thin. My grandmother lived to be 89—and with a broken hip the last 15 years of her life. She wouldn't go live with anybody. She lived on Washington Street, which was a leading section when she was young, but was practically down to nothing when she died. She wouldn't leave that area, though. My mother is 90 now, and as spirited and determined as she can be.

There were four sons and one daughter in my family. I was the baby. I was born December 26, 1924. My mother said she ate too much turkey on Christmas Day.

My three brothers are deceased now. O. T. Jr., was 10 years older than me and he died during an appendectomy operation when I was about four or five. I have no memories of him. Charles Edward, known as Huck, was 12 years older, and I expect my compulsion to be an athlete probably traces back to watching him play in high school when I was a small child. Huck was a fine football player. Bill Broyles was eight years older than me. Bill didn't participate in athletics. He went to work when he was about 13 years old, when the Depression started.

My sister, Louise, was five years older. She claims that she raised me. I think she claims it mostly to tease my mother; that's one of the jokes of the family. But Louise really was a benefactor when I was growing up. She took care of me and my spending money. When the war broke out, it was a tough time for us because the car business folded, and my daddy didn't have a job. Louise, who was working, helped support me through high school and bought my clothes.

Louise was an outstanding basketball player, maybe the best high school shooter they ever had in Decatur. She averaged 30 points a game. She was only five feet tall, but she could shoot the eyes out of it. I remember one time I scored more points in a grammar school game than she did in a high school game, and I couldn't wait to rush home and brag that I'd finally outscored my sister in basketball. She could play right along with the boys, our brothers, and the neighborhood kids in the backyard. Louise played semi-pro basketball five or six years after she got out of high school.

When I couldn't find a game of some kind, I often played baseball by myself. I'd take a ball and throw it against the side of the house and let it land for a base hit, or catch it for an out. I'd do that by the hour. In my mind it was the Yankees vs. the Red Sox. I liked the Red Sox, so they always won in my imagination.

The first time I went to see the Atlanta Crackers play I was no older than 11, and they had a camera day. My mother dug a little toy camera out of a Cracker Jacks box, and I was on my way. The Crackers' ball park was on Ponce de Leon, which ran right through Decatur and into Atlanta. I wanted to see the Crackers so desperately that I walked across town and started hitching a ride down Ponce de Leon Avenue. It was a six-mile trip. I was trotting down the street and thumbing for a ride and carrying my little toy camera—which was to be good for admission to the game. Somebody picked me up after a mile or two and took me to the ball park. My "camera" got me in free, but the game was rained out. So I hitchhiked back home. My family couldn't believe it.

I played my first organized ball in the fourth grade at Glenwood School. I did the punting barefooted. That's the way I'd learned to kick on the lot next to my home. I made the football team as the offensive center. I don't remember what I played on defense, but I know I punted from the start. In Decatur we had four grammar schools, and they played each other twice in everything during the school-year: football, basketball, and track. I also made the basketball team in the fourth grade.

About that time, we lost our home. We couldn't meet the taxes on the house my grandfather had given my father, where my family had lived close to 30 years. My grandfather owned two houses on

"Oakhurst was tough in 1937. In case you don't recognize me, I'm in the backfield second from your right."

Kings Highway, and the one at 115 was vacant. So we moved over there in 1935 and rented it from the realtor. It was considered a temporary arrangement at the time, but that remained our family home until my mother moved from Decatur in 1970.

Because of the change in address, I transferred to Oakhurst School, and that's where I first attracted attention as an athlete. In my seventh grade year, we won everything—football and basketball. I was much bigger than everybody else. We had a 105-pound limit in football, and I weighed right at 105. They always weighed me before a game. This sounds incredible, but I would score seven or eight touchdowns a game. They'd snap the ball to me, and I'd just run through everybody.

Georgia was on an 11-grade system in the public schools then: seven years in grade school and four in high school. There were no junior high programs as such. You went to high school in the eighth grade. So I was 13 years old and about to go to the eighth grade when one of the kids said; "Hey, Broyles. You're so big and good. Why don't you go out for the high school team?" I said, "Well, I plan to."

They all thought that was funny. Broyles is going out for the high school team, ha ha ha. I went out scared to death.

Boys' High of Decatur had only 25 players out for the football team, and naturally most of them were 10th and 11th graders. Because the squad was so small, they needed any willing eighth grader they could find. Our team was undefeated; they were called the 11 Iron Men. I wasn't one of those. I was a second-team blocking back, and I got to play in about three games. We were North Georgia Inter-Scholastic Conference champions, and as proud as we could be. We were challenged to go play Tyler, Texas, which had a great team but had been ruled out of the Texas high school playoff system because of some eligibility infraction. They inadvertently had left a kid's name off a list, and he had played, or something like that. Anyway, they felt frustrated and they weren't willing to end their season. I don't know how they found out about Decatur, Georgia, but they invited us over to Tyler and guaranteed our expenses.

We rode over there on a train. I remember waking up once when the train stopped, and somebody said we were in Texarkana. I was 13 years old, scared to death, and so far from home it was unreal. Tyler beat us about 37-0. You see, I found out about Texas teams a long time ago.

As soon as we got home, everybody jumped out for basketball. Our first game was against Clarkston, a little bitty town where they didn't play football; they'd been playing basketball for weeks. They had some great shooters and were running us ragged. The coach stuck me in as a substitute. I was all pumped up until I suddenly realized I didn't know which goal was ours. Boy, that's a funny feeling, running around out there, confused, trying to fake it, afraid to shoot.

In spite of that embarrassing start, I was considered a much better basketball player than football player in those days. Also, a much better baseball player than football player. And it was true that I had more talent to play those other sports at that time. But this went on right through my first two or three years at Georgia Tech, and it infuriated me even though I realized it was true.

Joe Martin, who had been a great end at the University of Georgia, was my coach at Boys' High in all sports. A fine man, a fine coach, but I'm sure he didn't find me too easy to handle. I know now that I was hard to coach. I was too big for my britches in my junior and senior years. I was spoiled; a little success had corrupted me a little bit. I had one or two run-ins with Coach Martin, particularly in baseball when he wanted me to pitch all the time. I was too good a hitter, I thought, to pitch. Just silly things.

I was a pretty good student—good enough to qualify for Tech, which wasn't easy—but I didn't work as hard at studying as I should have. In the sixth grade, I rebelled against one particular teacher and flunked two of her courses. I'd cut up in class, and she'd kick me out. I think it was history and geography. I had to repeat them in summer school, and when I was doing my homework, my mother would sit right over me, slapping my hands and cuffing me over the head when I slacked up. I never had to go to summer school again. I didn't really study except in study hall, because I always went to bed at 7:30. You had to take Latin in high school in those days. I had trouble with Latin, but who didn't?

I was a starter in basketball by the time I was 14. I turned 14 a few days after that bad outing in Clarkston, and I worked my way into the starting line-up before the season was over. I played guard and was a regular Sidney Moncrief for hawking the ball all over the court, stealing it, and taking it back in for lay-ups. Except, of course, I didn't attempt any of Sidney's slam dunks. Dunking the ball in those days was just an expression. You heard about it, but you almost never saw it. A man who could touch the rim was either a jumping jack or a giant. My junior and senior years, I played the post in basketball. I was bigger than most of them by far, could out-jump them all, and got a lot of points. I averaged 20 a game when our whole team averaged around 30.

In baseball, I was a lefthanded hitter and righthanded thrower. I pitched and played first base all spring for the high school, and all summer for the American Legion team, the Dekalb Barons. The Yankees were interested in signing me when I came out of high school, but although I still had vague plans to be a major league player, I knew I was going to college first.

By my senior year, I'd grown to 6-2, 180-85 pounds. That made me a big high school back for that day and time, and I don't think there's any doubt I had a big head to match. If my coach were alive, he'd tell you that.

During my sophomore year, they put me at blocking back. If there is one thing I wasn't, I wasn't very tough. I saw myself as a tailback: a runner, passer, and kicker. I'll never forget one week we were playing LaGrange, and Coach Martin moved me to end. I was mad because I didn't want to play in the line. But I played end. He saw I couldn't block at end, so I returned to be a blocking back. We had a good senior tailback, Ed Pierce, and I was hoping to replace him my junior and senior years. Which is the way it worked out.

We were a good football team, and we planned to win it all my senior season, 1941. We lost the second game of the year to Russell, 20-7, in a huge upset. Joe Martin really broke down and cried. It was the first time I had ever seen a coach cry, but I assure you it was not the last. We should not have lost that game. It knocked us out of the championship, and it knocked Martin out of an undefeated season. That was to be his last year. He was already planning to quit, but we didn't know it at the time. As it wound up, we lost one and tied one.

The public school system in Decatur had a Boys' High and a Girls' High, and between them was the gymnasium and library that served both schools. The boys and girls met in the library and passed notes back and forth, if they were lucky enough to go at the same time. I never started looking for excuses to go to the library until Barbara Day moved to Decatur during my junior year.

The schools were side by side, and the girls who lived on one side of town had to walk right in front of Boys' High going to Girls' High. That's where I first noticed Barbara; she was drawing a lot of wolf whistles and such from the boys. She also went to this dancing school. I didn't go to the dancing school, but I'd go by and hang around and watch them. One time this friend kept telling me I ought to ask her for a date. We found out she had a date on this particular Friday night, so I decided to ask her out that same night just to try to make an impression and build a little credibility for the future.

Well, I called and she said yes. I was in a pickle then, a real panic. I didn't have any money or a car or anything else. I thought she had forgotten she had a date with the other boy. Later I found out he called and broke the date before I called. Barbara thought I had persuaded him to break the date. "I thought that was real cute of you," she says.

I think I really fell in love with Barbara when I saw her at a Christmas dance in a white evening gown. We had our first date on January 24, 1942. It was a basketball night. She played for the Girls' High team, I played for the Boys', and we went out after the games.

We were together from then on, and most of our dating took place on a streetcar. Gasoline was rationed, and my family got a gallon and a half a week in rationing stamps; that was all.

The streetcar was a nickel. It ran right between our houses. She lived on Howard Street, which ran parallel to College, the main thoroughfare through Decatur. My home was four houses off College on the other side of the railroad track. So we lived about a block and a half apart, and the streetcar stopped right in front of her house. We could ride into Atlanta for a nickel and go to the movies. I cut lawns and caddied for a little movie money sometimes. Our dating consisted mostly of going for something to eat after football games, a movie in Decatur or Atlanta on Saturday night, and during basketball there was always a high school dance after home games.

I was 17 years old, and I didn't have much to be unhappy about. It bothered me that everybody said football was my worst sport, but I planned to rectify that as soon as possible.

3
YELLOWJACKETS AND BULLDOGS

In my time, Decatur was fertile University of Georgia territory. Boy, Georgia was on top. All you could hear from everybody in town was Georgia, Georgia, Georgia. Everybody except ole Frank! I was a Yellowjacket man in a world of Bulldogs. My family despised Georgia Tech, but I had that rebellious attitude. I was the Tech fan. There was never any doubt in my mind where I was going if I got a scholarship offer. Still, I went over to Georgia in the spring of my junior year of high school to work out with a group of other prospects. Schools could bring you in and try you out in those days. Scholarships were not very formal then, and recruiting rules, such as they were, were not enforced uniformly across the country. Anyway, the high school prospects lived in a dormitory with about 100 Georgia athletes, and I was scared to death. They were really a great football team. Most of their players were only two or three years older than us, I guess, but they seemed like men. We put on pads for a full-scale workout. I had a good day passing and kicking and they were apparently impressed. They recruited me heavily.

Tech did very little recruiting in those days. Georgia was bringing in 75 freshmen a year, and Tech might come up with 10 or 12. Georgia had been on the move since Wally Butts became head football coach in 1939. The 1930s hadn't been especially good to Tech coach Bill Alexander. All the momentum was over at Athens, definitely.

In addition to Georgia, I had scholarship offers from Duke and Clemson. The one I was waiting for, though, was relayed to me through Claude Bond, the Tech athletic trainer, who was a good friend of my daddy. Tech offered me a football scholarship sometime during my senior football season. I was thrilled, but they soon soured it for me. A couple of months later, during my senior basketball season, I was visited by Roy Mundorf, Tech's basketball and baseball coach. "Frank," he said, "we would like to offer you an exclusive. A baseball and basketball combination scholarship, and you don't play football." I took it as a real insult that he would think I'd give up football. I intended to go on playing all three sports, like I'd always done.

I guess everybody of a certain age can tell you where they were and what they were doing when they first heard the Japanese had attacked Pearl Harbor on December 7, 1941. I was playing touch football with a bunch of other high school kids on the campus of Emory University in Atlanta that Sunday afternoon. We went back to the car and turned on the radio and heard about Pearl Harbor. World War II was now a reality, not a rumor. I wondered how much, if any, time I would spend at Tech before I was inducted for military service.

The next spring I graduated from high school on a Friday night and enrolled as a Tech freshman the following Monday. Because of the war, the school went to an accelerated year-round program with a full semester in the summer. Jimmy Carter, a freshman from Plains, entered Tech at the same time. That's a fact I picked up a long time afterward. I didn't know him.

During that summer they held football practice two days a week, basketball practice two days a week, and that left two days for baseball—with Sunday open. Since I was a three-sport man I was practicing or playing six days a week.

Because of the war, college freshmen were declared eligible for varsity athletics. Tech was looking for a tailback because the only experienced returnee was Bobby Shelton, a 160-pounder with good instincts and intelligence but not much physical ability. They had to have somebody to alternate with him. The obvious candidates were me and Clint Castleberry, who'd been All-American everything at Boys' High in Atlanta.

The first day I worked at tailback, I threw four of the prettiest passes you've ever seen in your life, and I really got praised. I said to myself, "Boy, I'm gonna be on the varsity." Then I pitched a baseball game on a Saturday, and came back and practiced basketball the next Monday. Football practices were Tuesday and Thursday. When I got back to football the next Tuesday, my arm was dangling. I threw a couple of passes and, I give you my word, they went up and came down like the wounded dove of all wounded doves. That was the end of me on the varsity. They put me back and forgot about me. Only two freshmen made the varsity in the fall of '42: Castleberry and Bill Healey, a great lineman from Baylor Prep School at Chattanooga.

Every Monday that fall I'd go to my locker to see if I had a varsity jersey. I knew they just had to use me, but they never did. I never went to the varsity any time in my freshman season, not one day. I started for the basketball team as a freshman and I started for the baseball team as a freshman, but I was strictly a B-teamer in football. My critics, for the moment, were correct again.

Bobby Dodd used to tell people that in the 10 football seasons I was at Georgia Tech—four as a player and six as an assistant coach—we made 10 bowl trips. That's true, but all I did for that '42 team was help prepare them on the practice field.

William A. "Bill" Alexander, Coach Aleck, was only the second head football coach Georgia Tech had ever had. The first was John W. Heisman, for whom the Trophy is named. The first full-time, paid, professional coach, I mean. There was a football program of sorts before Heisman, because he was hired after one of his Clemson teams beat Tech by 73-0 in 1913. I've read that he moved to Tech for a $50 raise.

Heisman is credited with inventing the forward pass—or, at least, spotting its potential and campaigning for its legalization. He coached nearly 40 seasons at nine schools, starting in the 1890s, but his peak years were spent in Atlanta. He built national powerhouse teams at Tech around the time of World War I, and everything seemed rosy. Then in 1919 he and his wife got a divorce. Heisman told her that if she wanted to remain in Atlanta, he'd leave; if she wanted to leave, he'd stay. She decided she wanted to live in Atlanta, so Heisman went to Penn. Coach Aleck, who'd been his assistant coach, took over at Tech.

In his 25-year career, 1920-44, Coach Aleck went through some remarkable cycles of feast and famine. He had fine teams, generally, through most of the 1920s, but he went from 1929 to '37 without a winning season. When I knew him, he was an aging coach and rather controversial off the Tech campus. A certain faction had been sniping at him for years, partly because of those lean seasons and partly because he never stopped to worry about any enemies he might make. Even his friends and admirers conceded he was a gruff, tactless man. He held the total respect of his players because, no matter how much he berated them on the practice field, he really cared about them—and they sensed it.

Robert Lee "Bobby" Dodd was Coach Aleck's assistant, in charge of the backfield and the offense. I'll tell you much more about Dodd later. At the time I enrolled at Tech, he was plainly Coach Aleck's heir apparent. The '42 Tech team carried a 9-0 record into the Georgia game. It was obvious that the winner would go to the Rose Bowl— the Rose Bowl was still open to all teams in those days—and lo and behold, Tech was voted No. 1 in the country after a win over Notre Dame. Georgia was coming off a big upset at the hands of Auburn.

I don't guess any No. 1 team ever got beat the way we did that day in Athens. Castleberry was hurt on the first or second series, and they ran through us 34-0. Frank Sinkwich and Charley Trippi were never better. I didn't play, but I went to Athens to see the game. That was the lowest point. I thought Georgia Tech football would never survive.

Georgia went to the Rose Bowl and beat UCLA; Tech went to the Cotton Bowl and lost to Texas. And then everybody left. Almost all the Georgia team went into the service. Tech lost many, also, but we had the Navy training program as a block to build on. We lost three-fourths of our '42 squad, but because of the Navy program we added players from Vanderbilt, Alabama, and almost all the other Southeastern Conference schools. Everything turned around. We beat Georgia in 1943 48-0 and in 1944 44-0. To this day, Georgia followers refuse to acknowledge those two losses. They say they didn't lose to Georgia Tech; they sent a squad of 4Fs and freshmen against a Navy team that happened to be stationed at Tech.

Coach Aleck's offense was the single wing with an unbalanced line. I have to keep reminding myself there are adults around now who never saw a single wing team play, so I'd better brief you, just in case. The formation was "strong" to the side the wingback lined up on, left or right. The blocking back (and blocking was about all he did except on special plays) lined up close, to the left or right of the center, but not "under" center as with the T-formation quarterback. The ball was snapped back to the tailback or fullback; they lined up so that either could take a direct snap to start the play. Signals were

"Going into the 1943 season, I was a tailback candidate who could pass and kick."

ordinarily called by the tailback or the blocking back, but the job might go to any member of the backfield, depending on the coach's opinion of who had the best knowledge of the system and the best play-selecting instincts. We always had a quarterback, you see, in one form or another.

The old-time triple-threat hero (passer, runner, kicker) was usually the tailback, and he was usually the safety on defense as well in those one-platoon days.

Going into the 1943 season, I was a tailback candidate who could pass and kick. Eddie Prokop was a great ball carrier. He was the first 200-pound back I'd ever seen who could run 100 yards in less than 10 seconds flat. He'd played at Baylor Prep School, was a year ahead of me, and was really outstanding. So I couldn't believe it when I started at tailback ahead of him in the opening game against North Carolina. We won the game, 20-7, and Prokop came off the bench and starred.

We were on a train, going to play Notre Dame, when Bobby Dodd told me I was going to play wingback. I'd never practiced a day at wingback. "Well," Dodd said when I pointed that out, "get with Bobby Gaston (the regular wingback) and learn the plays." This was on a Thursday. All day Friday and all morning Saturday I was rehearsing the wingback plays. And I started and played the game at wingback.

Coach Aleck initiated a series with Notre Dame way back in Knute Rockne's time. "We won't beat 'em more than once out of 10," he said, "but we might learn something." The year before, when I was a freshman and not playing, Tech upset Notre Dame. The Irish had the best team in the country in '43, Frank Leahy's third year as coach, and they trampled us 55-13. But not right away. They had terrific athletes running the T-formation (Angelo Bertelli, Creighton Miller) but we stood in there for a half, 21-13. I kicked an extra point—the only score I ever made against Notre Dame.

Coach Aleck changed his defense at the half. We'd been playing a split six, three deep, and we went to a box defense, which was unheard of in those days. I was playing cornerback. I'll never forget. They had the end deep and a halfback in the flat. I'd go with the end, and they'd throw to the halfback. I'd cover the halfback, and they'd go to the end. I didn't know what I was doing, but whatever it was I knew it wasn't right. Notre Dame marched up and down the field the second half. They were national champions and looked like it.

I hurt my ankle chasing around between the halfback and the end, and was out for two weeks. When I came back, they put me at fullback. The newspapers started calling me Fireman Frank because I was always on call, ready to jump into a different position.

Prokop wasn't a passer. So at fullback, they would snap the ball to me if it was going to be a pass. Prokop would block, and I would throw. Otherwise, they'd snap the ball to Prokop, and he'd run. We went on and had a good year, 7-3.

Here's something I'll never forget. We were getting ready to play LSU, which had Steve Van Buren, later the great all-pro runner. Van Buren was a dangerous man returning punts. This was my first game after I came back from the ankle injury, and I'd just moved to fullback, alternating with a boy named Ed Scharfschwerdt. As I've told you, I always thought I could punt pretty well. But Scharfschwerdt—he was about 6-3 and a fine football player—could spiral that ball. He'd kick those beautiful line drives, and I was so embarrassed with my kicking. I mean, my ball would go high and end over end, about 38 or 40 yards at the most.

We were warming up for the LSU game, and Dodd walked over to me and said, "Frank, you're gonna start at fullback." Then he said, "You just keep kicking that way, and Van Buren won't return any of 'em." And he didn't, to speak of. All through my coaching career, that left an impression with me. It doesn't matter how far you kick it; you have to kick it where they can't return it. Hang time, they call it now.

We were picked to play Tulsa in the Sugar Bowl on January 1, 1944. Under Coach Aleck, Tech became the first school to make the rounds of the four major bowls. The Sugar Bowl bid completed the cycle; Tech teams had already visited the Rose, Orange, and Cotton bowls. Tulsa coach Henry Frnka had a famous team of 4Fs, kids who were draft-exempt for physical reasons. They even had a one-armed guard named Ellis Jones. Well, he was obviously a 4F.

On the first play of the game, we were going to throw a bomb to Phil Tinsley, our All-American end. Because of the element of surprise, Prokop was going to throw it. So the ball went to him and we thought we'd get behind their defense. Eddie never had a chance this time. The one-armed guard was all over him. When I got back to the huddle, he had blood all over his face (no face masks then.) Well, Prokop was a lady's man. He was a handsome youngster and loved the girls. Of course, he had some big plans for after the game, but there he was with his face puffing and blood all over him. "One

Armed Jones hit me right in the kisser," he said. "Gimme that gosh dern ball" (or words to that effect.)

We gave him the ball 25 times, which was unheard of for one game in those days, and he set a Sugar Bowl rushing record of 199 yards. We won 20-18. At the half, we were down, 18-7. Coach Aleck said very quietly, "If you want to have your party, fellows, you better go back out and win this one."

Like I said, Eddie had big plans.

I was playing halfback on defense, and when Tulsa tried to come back in the last minute they sent a man deep and a man short, and I was caught in the middle. They threw to the short receiver, and I came up and intercepted around our 15. We ran out the clock.

During spring practice in 1944, I seriously thought about giving up football for life. I had so much trouble with allergies that I would sneeze during practice to the point my nose would start bleeding. I just couldn't shake it. Sometimes I'd sneeze for 15 minutes without stopping. It bothered me for years until they learned how to control allergies, but it was worse that spring. Pollen and grass were the causes, but they didn't have anything to give me for it. I was probably the only player in America who carried a hankerchief on the field.

We had a good 8-2 season in '44, highlighted by a famous victory over Navy and low-lighted by a 19-13 loss to Duke and a 21-0 whipping at the hands of Notre Dame. Tech really had no business on the same field with Navy. The Academy had picked up All-Americans from schools all over the country (Army and Navy were the absolute cream of college football in '44 and '45), but we beat Navy 17-15 in one of the greatest games ever played in Atlanta—or anywhere. They were so much bigger and better than we were it was un-believable.

They went right through us at the start for a 6-0 lead. We got a break with a quick kick and took over on their eight-yard line. Our snap-count drew them offside, to the three. We punched it across in three tries for a 7-6 lead. They scored in about three plays, and it was 13-7. We intercepted a pass to set up an opportunity, and I threw a touchdown pass. We were back in front 14-13, but it was obvious we couldn't handle them physically. Except we did. They got to our two-yard line late in the fourth quarter, and we stopped them—four downs. We had a little guard, Squat Colbert, who didn't weigh 180 pounds, but I can still see him tearing into those huge Navy players like a demon.

Our tremendous goal-line stand defended a 17-15 lead, which proved to be the final score. They took a 15-14 lead with a safety. Late in the fourth quarter, freshman Allen "Dinky" Bowen, one of our all-time great running backs, kicked the field goal that made the difference for us. About three plays after the field goal, they were raging around down inside our five, and we stopped them. How in the world, I'll never know.

The last play of the game was a deep pass to Clyde Scott, the Navy star from Smackover, Arkansas, the fastest man in college football and later the vital post-war recruit who would start John Barnhill's program at Arkansas. We knew how fast Clyde was, and I was covering him deep on the last play. I did something that I've spent the rest of my life coaching against. I intercepted the pass, tried to run it back, and fumbled it. Navy recovered, but the game was over. Coach Aleck and Dodd really lit into me, and from that time on, when we intercepted late in a game, we got on the ground in a hurry. It became kind of a joke among us. "Touch your knee down and then run like the devil."

Ben Martin, the Air Force coach, played for Navy that day. Years later, at one of our coaches' golf tournaments, Barbara and I were sitting around one night with Ben and his wife and John McKay and his wife, and we got to talking about the Tech-Navy game of 1944 from three viewpoints. It sounded like three different games. Ben told his version of it, and I told my version. McKay had been in the stands. He was stationed at the Navy Pre-flight School at Athens and he came over to watch the game. He remembered it in a completely different way. We laughed all night. I guess there are at least three sides to every game.

My blocking was so atrocious in our loss to Duke that, after we looked at the film on Monday, I got benched—the only time in my life. I learned first-hand what a blow it is to a starter's pride, and every time I had to bench a player later on, I remembered what went through my own mind in 1944. I'll have to admit my blocking was so bad it was unreal. I was benched for the Tulane game, and we were struggling along, needing to pass, and finally Dodd put me in. I threw four touchdown passes for a Georgia Tech record, and we won 34-7. My blocking also picked up considerably.

We played LSU in front of a big and typically hostile crowd at Baton Rouge. The Tigers were mostly freshmen (including Y. A. Tittle), and they were tough kids. We had to sweat very earnestly for a 7-6 lead. We stopped them inside our one-yard line, and I lined up in punt formation in the end zone. Dodd was far ahead of his time. In those days, if you threw an incomplete pass or grounded the ball behind the goal-line, you were penalized half-the-distance to the goal. That rule has since been changed. We had a drill where we'd get a bad snap behind the goal line, and we'd pick up the ball and throw it out of the end zone. You just did that automatically.

Well, we were kicking on third down from our end zone, and the ball hit me right in the hands, popped right out, and dropped to the ground, the only time in my career that I can remember that happening to me on a punt. Instinctively, because of the practice we'd had, I grabbed the ball and threw it up in the stands.

You talk about booing, I never heard anything to equal it. They penalized us six inches and when we snapped the ball on fourth down, I kicked it out. The booing never stopped the rest of the game.

George Matthews was our freshman wingback, and he liked to "hide out." When we were making substitutions, he'd follow three or four replaced players off the field, except he'd stay in bounds in front of the Tech bench, sort of lost in the crowd. We had a signal for it, call "Benny." If Matthews was hid out, "Benny, Benny" meant line up quick and snap the ball to me, and I'll throw it to George.

We were making a few player moves to receive an LSU punt, and George trotted by me, saying, "Frank, I'm gonna hide out." But George ran off the wrong way, to the wrong side of the field. He was "hiding" right in front of the LSU student body. Everybody in the stands on that side jumped up, yelling and pointing to him, trying to get the attention of the players on the LSU bench. I was in the huddle yelling "Benny! Benny!" and our players were just looking at me. By now, it sounded like everybody in the stands was about to come storming out on the field. I started yelling, "Matthews is hiding out over there. Line up and snap it!" The LSU players could have heard me if their fans hadn't been making so much noise. I threw to George and he scored, and they really screamed bloody murder then. We won 14-6, but I didn't think we'd get out of Baton Rouge alive.

Against Notre Dame, I was knocked out cold for the only time in my life. I was blocking the end on an off-tackle play, and I got my "bell rung." I don't know how to explain it, but I was hit on the head and wound up with a hip injury. I was woozy most of the game, and when my mind cleared up I realized I had a hip-pointer. We were getting ready to play Georgia, in Athens, and Tech hadn't won at Athens in a long time. I wasn't sure I could play against Georgia because of the hip, but I had probably the best game I ever had. I completed 24 out of 34 passes for 350 yards. I scored two touchdowns and passed for three. Georgia had all freshmen and sophomores and 4Fs, and we beat them 44-0. Georgia was penalized six times for slugging me during the game. Johnny Lynch, an official from New Orleans who was in the game, dropped the flag on Georgia 15 times. He never called a Georgia game after that.

The Orange Bowl put us against Tulsa, a rematch of the previous Sugar Bowl. Coach Aleck told us just before the Orange Bowl game he was retiring as coach. I think we all sensed he was near retirement, but the idea that this was his last game made us all cry. We desperately wanted to let him go out as a winner, but we weren't up to it. Tulsa had a stronger, more mature football team than the one we beat at New Orleans. They put it on us 26-12.

Dinky Bowen was our runner. He had hurt his knee in the Georgia game and could play only a little bit at Miami. We knew we couldn't have a balanced offense, so on the first play I lined up and quick-kicked the ball. That old side-winder kick we used, end over end, went about 55 or 60 yards. They didn't return it. Tulsa lined up and Perry Moss, who was outstanding at Illinois after the war, quick kicked it right back to us. The Orange Bowl opened with two quick kicks, and I'd guess it was the only time in the history of football anything like that happened. All we could do was throw the ball. We passed for 304 yards and rushed for 36. I threw for 279 yards, which was the Orange Bowl record for a long time. Joe Namath of Alabama broke it against Texas.

At first, my mother wasn't going to the Orange Bowl game. My daddy went down with some other people to see the game and do some fishing, and then my mother changed her mind. She advertised in one of the Atlanta papers, "I'm Frank Broyles' mother and I want a ride to Miami to see the game." A young couple called up and said sure, she could ride. She slept in the back seat and reached Miami before daddy got there. Barbara was in the group traveling with my daddy. During the Orange Bowl week I asked her to marry me, and we bought the ring as soon as we got back to Atlanta.

We would have married sooner, but Coach Aleck wouldn't allow me to be married, and also the Navy program wouldn't allow me to be married. You couldn't be married in the Navy until you received your commission, and I expected to be commissioned within the next few months.

During the 1944 season, Dodd started calling me a "coach on the field." I was no longer sensitive about my football ability; I was named Southeastern Conference player of the year. My player-of-the-year trophy was to be conferred at a banquet, but it looked like I couldn't go. Because of something that happened, some breakdown in discipline, everybody in the Navy unit at Georgia Tech was confined to the campus. At the last minute, Bosh Pritchard (who later played for the Philadelphia Eagles and was then a Navy PE instructor) worked it out where he could take me to the banquet to receive my trophy.

They handed it to me and the top fell off. I hoped it wasn't an omen of some kind.

4
WAR STORIES

My daddy always said I was the luckiest person that ever lived. He'd rather have my luck than a million dollars. Bobby Dodd, my coach, was fond of saying, "If you think you're lucky, you are." When I look back on a series of events in my life during the war years, I have no choice but to conclude that I'm lucky.

Toward the end of the summer of '42, with the war going badly, people in school worried that they couldn't finish their education and get their officer rank before they had to go. Coach Aleck came in and told everybody that the Air Force (it was still the Army Air Corps then) was going to leave its people in school until they graduated. Then they'd go to flight school, get their commissions, and become pilots. He said he had inside information from Washington. He recommended that everybody join the Air Corps.

Well, I did *NOT* want to be in the Air Corps. About half our football team signed up, but I didn't. That was in August. About mid-September, Coach Aleck said the Army had also agreed that it would leave its reserve people in school until they got their degrees, then they would go to Officer Candidate School. He urged that those who passed up the Air Corps join the Army's Enlisted Reserve Corps (ERC) or the Navy reserves. The Navy had also promised to maintain its on-campus program, but I didn't want any part of the Navy, either.

The Army appealed to me. I'd been an ROTC captain in high school, and I liked to drill. I had that forceful HUT . . . TWO . . . THREE . . . FOUR. I figured I'd join the Army reserves. I took my time. I wouldn't be 18 until December 26, so about the first of December, I went in to join the ERC. It was closed; they wouldn't take any more. I was then in a state of shock. The Navy was all I had left. I enlisted in the Navy Reserves on December 23. Around the last week in January of 1943, they called every Air Corps reserve, put them on active duty and shipped them out to flight school.

Around the second week of February, the Army called up every ERC student. Everybody was walking around saying, "Well, the Navy's next." The Navy came out with an announcement that it was going to leave its people in school. All my buddies who had joined the Air Corps were gone. The Army had gone. I didn't want the Navy but I had to take it. The Navy let me stay at Georgia Tech five more semesters.

I put on the seaman's uniform, drew about $35 or $50 a month in military pay, and went on to school. At the end of the spring semester, I had orders to report to Emory University. So did Eddie Prokop and Mickey Logan. We were to be the starting tailback, fullback, and wingback at Georgia Tech the next fall. For some reason, the Navy dispatched all its industrial management majors to Emory. Engineering was the only alternative field at Tech.

Naturally, we went running to Coach Aleck. "You go on over to Emory," he said, "and I'll take care of it." On about June 5, we reported to Emory. On about June 7, we were transferred back to Georgia Tech, and all three of us signed up for civil engineering. All my electives, though, were in industrial management.

I stayed at Tech until March 20, 1945. I played basketball all the way through, along with football, and I left from Louisville, Kentucky, after our team was knocked out of the Southeastern Conference tournament. The tournament was always at Louisville, because Kentucky was the best team and the best drawing card.

I got on an airplane for the first time in my life and flew from Louisville to Providence, Rhode Island, to take officer training at the Mid-Shipman's School. I remember landing at Washington en route, and was scared to death when we started coming down. I changed planes at New York, and felt just a little bit more at ease in a DC-3. The Providence weather was cold and miserable, but that was the least of my worries. They stuck me in a fast Mid-Shipman's School, and I wasn't coping too well. I hadn't done much in the Navy except wear the uniform and go to class. Well, they carried me too fast. Most of the cycles were three months, but they were trying to cram us through in six weeks. They were hammering away at me about navigation. I thought navigation meant following your blockers.

Well, for the third and last time in my life, I kind of rebelled against academic authority. I've told you about the incident in the sixth grade. Then, at Georgia Tech in '43, some of us let our grades slide and started saying, "Aw, we're gonna go fight anyway. Might as well get it over with." Coach Aleck called me in and straightened me out that time, but I felt the same way at Mid-Shipman's School. I sort of gave up. Then I became desperate. Barbara and I were to be married in May. The wedding invitations said "Ensign Frank Broyles." I was afraid she was going to have to cross out "Ensign."

For three weeks I flunked test after test. Then the commander of the school called me on the carpet.

"Broyles," he said, "you've got officer potential, but if you don't get busy, you're going straight to boot camp."

Somehow, I did an about face and pulled away from being among the 15 or so they were going to bust out at the bottom. I studied all night sometimes; it was the first time in my life I'd really studied. I finished about 40th in a class of 126. I received my commission at 11 a.m., on Saturday, May 5. Barbara and I were to be married at 6:30 p.m., Sunday, May 6—except I was in Rhode Island and she was in Georgia, and we had a lot of wartime travel complications in between.

I was booked on a train out of Providence, and a connecting train in New York was supposed to get me to Atlanta at 4:15 Sunday afternoon. Most trains ran late in those days. One of my buddies suggested we go over to the Naval Air Station and try to hook a ride. Sure enough, about six of us caught a DC-3 going to LaGuardia Airport at New York. You could hitch-hike on military aircraft, but you couldn't fly commercial without special permits. So I figured I was ahead of the game now. If I couldn't get another air ride, I'd go to the train station and fill my original schedule. While we were sitting in the LaGuardia terminal, a guy came through and said he was going to the Marine base at Quantico, Virginia. He only had room for one, and an Army private was ahead of me.

My buddy walked over to him and said, "Say, this fellow has got to get married. He's about to miss his wedding. Would you let him take this flight?" The private looked me over, in my brand new little ensign's uniform, and finally said, "Yeah, sure." So I thanked him and

walked out there and saw a little two-seated trainer plane. I was
scared to death, but I had no choice. I loaded my luggage and
climbed in the seat behind the pilot. He handed me a parachute and
showed me where to pull. Well, I'd read Drew Pearson, the Washington columnist, religiously from the time I was in high school. He'd
been writing a series of articles about Navy pilots who had drowned
because they couldn't get rid of the parachute when they bailed out
over water. I thought about Drew Pearson and the parachutes while
we were humming along over Chesapeake Bay.

Just before we took off, the trainer pilot turned to me and tried to
tell me how to hook up my microphone so I could talk to him. I
couldn't find the place to hook it up. We were flying along, with me
intently listening for the engine to skip a beat, when I realized the
pilot was gesturing, trying to communicate with me. I shrugged.
Then he handed me a piece of paper, and I grabbed it and read:
JUMP INSTRUCTIONS. You talk about nearly passing out. I fran-
tically read the jump instructions, trying to summon enough nerve
to jump. I yelled at him, but you couldn't hear a thing over the engine noise. He kept waving, and finally it dawned on me he was
indicating that I should turn the paper over. On the other side, he
had scribbled instructions about plugging in the intercom so we
could talk. The jump instructions sheet was the only piece of paper
he could find. I didn't know if I should laugh or cry. I was about five
seconds away from jumping when I finally figured everything out.

We landed at Quantico, and nothing was coming in. My only
chance was to get to Washington and try to catch a train.

By then, it was late Saturday afternoon. I called the railroad lines,
and found that the old Southern had a train going through, from
New York to Atlanta, due out of Washington at eight that night. It
was booked solid, but they said there might be come cancellations.
That was my last hope.

The Quantico Marines were storming into Washington for the
weekend. Limousine drivers would come out to the base, pack six or
eight Marines into a limo, and haul them to Washington at three
dollars a head. I crowded into one of the cars, paid the fee, and we
took off over the first big interstate highway I'd ever seen. The
Marines in my car started goading the driver: "We've got to get to
town, man. See how fast you can go." He didn't need much encour-
agement; he was already doing 80 miles an hour. In a few seconds, he

Ensign and Mrs. Frank Broyles, May 6, 1945.

was flying along at 110. I was more scared than I'd been in the trainer plane. "Hey, don't drive so fast," I pleaded. "I'm going to get married." The Marines laughed and egged him on. We blasted into Washington like a rocket.

There had been a few cancellations, so they let me on the train. I reached Atlanta at nine o'clock Sunday morning. Barbara came to the train station, which was a terrible breach of wedding day tradition. We checked later on the train I originally considered catching and it reached Atlanta at 10 that night. I would have missed my wedding.

The next day Barbara and I caught a train back to Rhode Island, where I had to go for some post-commission training. We had a compartment. When we stopped in New York, we realized a big celebration had broken out. Germany had offered to surrender, it was V-E (Victory in Europe) Day. "You see," I told Barbara, "the Germans heard Broyles got his commission. They threw in the towel."

After a couple of months at Providence and a couple of weeks' leave, Barbara and I caught a crowded troop train to San Francisco, where I expected to be stationed the next two or three months. I was standing in a line to report, and an officer said the next 60 people that checked in were going to fly immediately to Hawaii. I reached San Francisco on a Monday, and I was to leave on Wednesday.

Poor Barbara. We spent four days traveling west on the train, and she had to turn around and head right back. We had become close friends with another Navy couple, Leland and Mary Jane Karr, who were in the same situation. Leland and I were together in line when we were picked for Hawaii. Barbara spent a few days at Minneapolis with Mary Jane on the way home. They headed east on a troop train with 4000 Marines who were going home after two or three years overseas. Barbara said it was a much happier train than the one we came out on.

While we were in San Francisco, we heard about the first atomic bomb being dropped at Hiroshima. We flew to Hawaii, checked into the barracks at Pearl Harbor, and the next thing you know a wild celebration broke out. This was August 14, 1945, and the Japanese had agreed to surrender. When we heard all the shouting at Pearl Harbor, we thought it was another Japanese raid. I've always said they heard I was coming and quit.

We were to have been part of the invasion force for Tokyo, and now they had to find things to do with us. After two or three weeks in Hawaii, I flew to Guam and then Okinawa, where I would eventually have gone in any case. Now I was 8000 or so miles from home, I had been in the Navy three years, and I'd still never seen the inside of a ship.

I reached Okinawa just in time for the great typhoon of October 9, the worst storm they'd ever had there. I was sitting in a tent over Buckner Bay looking down the cliffs at the ships and listening to radio information about the storm. My roommate, who'd been checking around outside, stuck his head in and said, "Hey, come out here, Frank." We were the only ones in the area. I couldn't see a soul. About that time, our tent went over the cliff. We hid behind a jeep nearly an hour, which we realized wasn't too smart, so we edged our way over to an old Japanese cave we knew about. The water seeped in up to my waist before we had to leave. I wasn't hurt at all, but we went to the hospital to see if we could help move the injured or anything, and it was there that I drank a cup of coffee for the first time in my life. My mother wouldn't let me drink anything but lemonade and buttermilk when I was growing up. Barbara finally corrupted me; she introduced me to iced tea.

A commander of recreation and sports events had enough points to go home, but he couldn't get a release until they found a replacement. When he found out I was an athlete, he talked the base commander into letting me replace him. I was 20 years old with a big office and a clerk and a secretary, and I didn't have the faintest idea of what to do. "Let's start some baseball games," I said. After a few days, my buddy Leland Karr came in and whispered that the commander had received a wire instructing him to send all ensigns with no assignments back to Pearl Harbor. They were deactivating units right and left, and people were going and coming all the time. Leland worked in personnel. "Would you like to go?" he asked. "Put me on that list, Buddy," I said.

Eight of us ensigns got ready to leave. I hadn't been in Okinawa a month, and I was headed back. I got on a ship for the first time, a big tanker, and the captain said, "Hey, we've got orders to send y'all back." He stood there grinning at eight stunned ensigns.

"What are you going to do?" I finally asked.

"What would you like for me to do?" he said.

"We're already on here," I said. "Let's just take off."

The captain pondered for a second or two, and laughed. "Okay, we'll do that."

I was seasick all the way back to Pearl Harbor. I reported to the officer who was to decide what I was going to do next, and, lo and behold, he was the old Georgia Tech track coach, George Griffin. "Broyles," he roared, "what in the world are you doing back here? What in the world are we gonna do with y'all?" He wired Washington, and the instructions were to discharge everybody who had enough points, and send the rest to Johnson Island. Johnson Island was a speck in the middle of the equator where we had some Seabee battalions.

"Coach Griffin," I said, "If you count my points of being overseas

"My little ensign's uniform was as fresh and unadorned as it was the day I had come out of Providence. . . ."

for the next two months, I'll have enough points to go home." While he was trying to figure the logic in that, I added, "Besides, spring practice is going to be starting pretty soon." He ruled that I had enough points to go home.

Right after Christmas, I got transportation on the aircraft carrier *Saratoga*. There were seven or eight thousand returning soldiers, sailors and Marines on there, and they were sacked out all over the decks and everywhere. Most of them were combat veterans. My little ensign's uniform was as fresh and unadorned as it was the day I had come out of Providence: no ribbons or stripes signifying campaigns or tours of duty. Everybody kept asking me, how could I be going back home? "Battlefield promotion," I said. That was all I could think of.

Barbara and I met in Knoxville, and, although we love Knoxville, it wasn't the ideal place to have your second honeymoon. I remained in the Navy until the next February, but the last few weeks were spent as a PE instructor at Georgia Tech. My buddy, Leland Karr, ended up on Johnson Island.

So that was my career in the Navy. The decisions that were forced

on me or that I fell into turned out to be the right ones. Clint
Castleberry, the great freshman back, one of the finest athletes ever
to enroll at Georgia Tech, was killed in the war. He'd gone in the Air
Corps, along with many others. Some of my other teammates and
friends had died in service.

There's no way around it. I was the luckiest of the lucky.

5
THE "T" AND I

Unless you were there, you can't imagine the way college football was in 1946 with all the veterans back from the war. Many schools had a 90 percent personnel turnover from the previous fall. With all that talent available, life was very real and earnest on the practice field.

As I look back, the Navy program had really saved Georgia Tech football and set up the prosperous years of the late 1940s and early 1950s. We were on our way down just before the war and had just about given up competing equally with Georgia, Tennessee, and the others. We came out of the war under a full head of steam.

As everyone had anticipated, Bobby Dodd moved up to head coach in 1945 while I was away, and installed the Chicago Bears' T-formation, which had become the rage of football. Tech had just a so-so year in '45—4-6—because the Navy people were gone by then. T-quarterback seemed perfect for me as I was basically a passer, ball-handler, and kicker and not much of a runner. The quarterback wasn't called on to carry the ball much in the old standard T.

During a Tuesday practice two and half weeks before our opening game with Tennessee, Dodd and backfield coach Ray Ellis, and an Atlanta *Journal* writer, Morris McLemore, were needling me about my blocking. That had been a real sore spot with me ever since I'd been benched that time for my futile blocking. I'll show 'em, I thought.

We had a scrimmage going, and we were right in front of where the three of them were sitting on a bench. I called the only play that required me to block. I turned and pitched the ball for a sweep on which the quarterback led the play. It was the same play Jon Brittenum got hurt on in the Cotton Bowl game against LSU 20 years later. I was really going to wipe out that B-team cornerback, leave him right at the feet of Dodd, Ellis, and McLemore. He backed away from the block, and I fell on my shoulder and completely separated it.

You talk about being sick. I still had some illusions of a baseball career, but I knew that was gone out the window. The team doctor convinced me I could play football without an operation, and I grabbed at that because it was my senior season. The orthopedic surgeons who did all the work for Georgia Tech pleaded with me to have an operation. I never did, and I've still got a knot back there.

On Saturday, after I was hurt on Tuesday, they filled the shoulder with novacaine, taped and braced it as best they could, and I went out and tried to throw the football. I could throw it 10 or 15 yards, but it hurt. The next week, I could throw 25 or 30 yards. I didn't start against Tennessee, but I was in there by the middle of the first quarter. We were on our 15-yard line and the defense was crowding, forcing, coming up with everybody. I'll show 'em, I said. I called a bomb to our left end. I threw the ball and—I can see it right now—I thought it was going to come right back to me. They intercepted and took it in to score, but we marched the length of the field and went ahead, 7-6. I was taken out, and Tennessee eventually won it on another pass interception, 13-9. We went on to a good year, 8-2, and beat St. Mary's in the Oil Bowl 41-19. St. Mary's and the Oil Bowl have both disappeared from big-time football.

In the Duke game, a 14-0 win for us, I had my best kicking day ever. I punted dead inside the Duke five-yard line three times. Coach Aleck, then the Tech athletic director, came by afterward and said, "Frank, I've been looking at Wallace Wade's teams for 25 years, and that's the first time I ever saw him get beat by the kicking game."

We played Duke in the mud, and by the third play you couldn't tell one Tech player from another. Except me. My teammates were covered in slush from their shoes to their helmets, and I was as spotless as if I were posing for a yearbook picture. I handed off and threw a few little short passes, and played safety on defense. Duke's offense was going nowhere, so I didn't have any work at safety. The team nearly died laughing when we looked at the film on Monday. I've never lived that down.

In spite of my clean uniform, my injured shoulder was "stung" in the Duke game, and I didn't start against Navy. We jumped out ahead of them 14-0, and then, all of a sudden, they turned on us and just beat the devil out of us. I mean they just wore us out. The scoreboard didn't look too bad, 20-14, but anybody who was there knows they dominated us most of the game. It was so one-sided I promise you no more than 3000 people were in the stands at the finish.

Late in the fourth quarter, Navy was on our two-yard line, ready to jam over another touchdown. Their fullback went sailing over the top and our linebacker, Johnny McIntosh, hit him and the ball squirted up in the air. George Matthews caught it and went 98 yards to score. We kicked the extra point. We were dying a few seconds before, but then we were ahead 21-20. We kicked off, they started a desperation passing attack, and Pat McHugh intercepted and ran the ball down to their eight. Just a few seconds remained.

Dodd ran over and grabbed me. "Okay, Frank," he said. I had not been in the ball game. I suppose I was stuck in at that point because Dodd wanted an experienced senior to handle the ball and run out the clock. I was so surprised that I didn't hit the field in a very clear-headed state. George Brodnax, an end, stuck his head in the huddle and said, "Bootleg." Asleep at the switch, sort of, I called the bootleg pass. The team didn't want to run it, but they didn't say anything.

I thought Dodd called it from the bench; I thought Brodnax was bringing in a play. That was my argument later, anyway. I just didn't think at the time. In the film, you can see our three backs didn't bother to fake at all. They just backed up to protect against a pass interception—to keep somebody from running the length of the field. They were in the game; I wasn't. I took two steps, jumped up, and threw a touchdown pass to Brodnax. We won 28-20 instead of 21-20.

That was the worst call by a Georgia Tech quarterback for all time, but Broyles was lucky again. I'm not sure Brodnax would own up to saying, "bootleg," and I never had the nerve to ask him about it. To this day, if you mention my name to one of my 1946 teammates he'll start telling you within 10 seconds about the bootleg pass against Navy while we were trying to play it safe and kill the clock.

The Southeastern Conference had two quarterbacks, Charley Conerly of Ole Miss and Y. A. Tittle of LSU, who later were legendary NFL winners. For a pretty good piece of trivia, I was picked on the All-SEC team ahead of them, probably because we beat both of them. Ole Miss wasn't very good that year, but LSU (the LSU squad that played a scoreless tie with Arkansas in the 1947 Cotton Bowl) lost only to us. We beat them in Baton Rouge, where something really wild always happened. This time they turned out the lights while Tommy Carpenter was running back a pass interception. This was homecoming, and they were going to shoot cannons, firecrackers, and everything. We were leading 20-7, and they turned out the lights before he reached the end zone. The officials awarded the touchdown, and we won by 26-7. When the lights went out, the cannons started booming, and the people in the stands ran out on the field. I thought we were all going to be killed.

We took an 8-1 record into the Georgia game at Athens, where we caught Charley Trippi closing his senior year. Trippi was more than ready for us; he scored four times on fourth down and they won 35-7. This game taught me a lesson about gimmick offenses. We were going to line up in a balanced T-formation and shift to an unbalanced set. Georgia had a tackle, Bulldog Williams, who jumped offside the first eight times we tried it. I called it every third down. Georgia fans booed us every step of the way as we went in for a 7-0 lead. Finally, the Georgia defense started showing a little patience with our shift, and they wiped us out.

I must tell you about my punt return against Tulane. That ranks with my clean jersey in the Duke game and my last-second call against Navy. Ordinarily, I didn't return kicks. In a punt receiving situation, Dinky Bowen and George Matthews would drop back, and I'd move up to halfback. Otherwise I played safety. Tulane quick-kicked, catching me at safety. I picked up the ball around the 15-yard line and started running. T-formation quarterback was a rocking chair position in those days, and I wasn't in the greatest shape. I reversed my field a couple of times, kept circling, looking, backtracking, and ran well over 100 yards getting to the end zone. I was so tired I fell on my face as I crossed the goal line.

The jokes started right there. Some of my teammates claimed they blocked three men. Some of them said they blocked the same man three or four times. They said they'd block somebody, then get up and run to block somebody else. Somebody called it the longest run in history—in elapsed time. Dodd tells the story that they called it back for delay of the game. Actually it was called back because of a clipping penalty. After all that running, it didn't even stand as an official play.

I'll still tell you I was slow. I haven't become an All-American 35 years after the fact—like some of them.

6
WOODRUFF'S NEOPHYTE

I can't pinpoint the time I first wanted to coach. I'm sure the beginnings of it were in the 1944 season when Bobby Dodd started telling people I was a "coach on the field." I know I started thinking earnestly about it in '46 after I hurt my shoulder. A career in professional baseball, my earliest dream, was out of the question. The Chicago Bears were interested in me as a quarterback, but I knew I'd always be a limited passer because of the injury. As I played out the Georgia Tech basketball season of 1946-47, I fretted about my future. I had two more years of eligibility. They didn't count the two seasons I played at Tech while I was in the Navy. Dodd probably wanted me to come back as a player in '47, but he wasn't emphatic about it. I'm not sure what Dodd's feelings were. Moreover, I wasn't certain I wanted to play another football season.

Bob Woodruff was Dodd's line coach in '46. He was a University of Tennessee product, like Dodd, and he'd come from West Point to give us a great defensive record. Baylor University hired him as head coach early in '47. Dodd interviewed for the job, turned it down, and Baylor swung to Woodruff. When I heard that, I asked Ray Ellis, the Tech backfield coach, if he'd talk to Woodruff about a job for me at Baylor. Freshman coach, or something like that. Ellis wouldn't take me seriously. "You don't want to coach," he said. "Not yet. You're gonna come back and play for us."

The Bears drafted me, and I dickered with coach George Halas all through basketball season. I knew if I played any more football, it was going to be in the pros. After settling in at Waco, Woodruff came for his family and dropped in for a goodbye visit with Dodd. Bob saw me and called me over. "Frank, how'd you like to come over during spring vacation and work with my kickers?" he asked.

"Bob, I've been trying to find you," I said. "I'm not going back. I want a job. I'm gonna play pro ball."

Bob started whispering. "Look, don't say anything about it. Would you really like to come and coach? I'll hire you as backfield coach."

"Bob, that's a dream come true," I said. I was flabbergasted. "I just want to be the freshman coach. I just want to get started."

"Don't say anything," he repeated. "I'll call you next Wednesday night."

At the appointed time, the phone rang. "I've got it all worked out," Woodruff said. "At the end of basketball season, you go on and sign with the Bears. Then I'll call Dodd and say I read that in the paper, and ask him if he thinks Frank would like to be a coach. And he'll say, 'Why, he ought to be a coach. He can't make it in pro ball.' Don't worry about a thing, Frank. It'll be all right."

Any Southeastern Conference basketball race was a foregone conclusion in those days. The only suspense involved who might finish second to the Kentucky Wildcats; Adolph Rupp's teams were the class of the country, as well as the conference. Going up against Alex Groza, Wah-Wah Jones, Ralph Beard, etc., was a humbling experience indeed. In my time, Tech was usually in the fight for second place. We never beat Kentucky, but we made it close a time or two, and Rupp used to get on me something fierce during the games. I can hear him now. "BROYLES! BROYLES! GET OFF HIM! This isn't football, Broyles. Quit holding him." I was a guard in college basketball, although Coach Rupp evidently thought I was a linebacker. I heard his commentary for the last time in March of 1947. We were knocked out of the conference basketball tournament on a Saturday, and the Sunday papers carried the story that I would sign with the Chicago Bears that day.

Monday, Dodd called me in. "Frank, I was just talking to Bob Woodruff," he said. "You don't want to play pro ball. Not with the Bears. They've got Sid Luckman, and Johnny Lujack's on the way. No. 3 quarterback, punter, that's the best you can hope for. You know you're going to coach sometime. Why don't you go right into it?"

"Do you think Woodruff would hire me?" I asked.

"Sure. He called. He's interested. Call him back."

"I was a guard in college basketball, although Coach Rupp evidently thought I was a linebacker."

Actually, Woodruff wasn't tampering. Bob never mentioned a full-time job to me until I assured him I was through playing at Tech. He figured Dodd would never believe that, though, so we used the Bears' contract as a smokescreen.

I'd just turned 22, and my age would be a source of considerable confusion for a long time. The newspaper articles about me signing with the Bears said I was 21. When I went to Baylor, I moved my age up to 25. I'd be coaching war veterans who were 22, 23, 24. I bought a hat so I'd look older, and fudged my age up to 25, but some of our players were older than my alleged age. Barbara says that later on I had to remain 29 three years in a row to let my true age catch up with me. That's about the way it was.

I was scared, naturally. I'd never coached; everything was new. When I got to Waco I found that Bob Woodruff and I basically were the coaching staff. Bill Henderson, the basketball coach, worked with the ends a little bit. Uncle Jim Crow, bless his soul, was the B-team coach and equipment manager. I walked in and Woodruff told me, "I want you to coach the backs just like Dodd coached you.

I'll handle the line." That's all he said. Then he assigned me the job of charting films of the past two years. I charted every play of the offense and defense on every film, and that's when I started to realize how fascinating football really was and how much there was to learn. The offenses of SMU, TCU, and Texas A&M scared me to death. They were throwing 40 and 50 passes a game from the spread, the double wing, and the triple wing.

"Bob, I don't know anything about this," I said one day.

"We'll play three deep," he said. "If it doesn't work, we can get fired awfully fast.'

Well, no one in the Southwest Conference was playing that way against a spread. They were trying to use some form of "man" coverage on all the receivers. What we played amounted to a "prevent" defense at all times, because we regarded the spread as a long-yardage formation. On obvious passing downs, we rushed three men. The more passes they completed, the fewer men we rushed and the more we dropped back, and so forth. I'm not sure any of the passing teams ever threw for a touchdown on us—a critical touchdown, I mean—and by the time Bob and I left Baylor, the spread was nothing. Everybody was playing prevent defense against it, all over the field and all through the game.

In my first few weeks as a coach, I was strictly a demonstrator. I'd work with the quarterbacks, running through all the hand-offs myself, and passing and punting. I could throw better than any of the passers and kick better than any of the kickers until we got Adrian Burk. When I saw him kick a ball 25 yards longer than I had ever kicked one in my life, I decided never to punt in his presence again. The Southwest Conference was dominated by tough, shrewd, legendary coaches: Matty Bell at SMU, Dutch Meyer at TCU, Jess Neely at Rice, John Barnhill at Arkansas, Homer Norton at Texas A&M, and Dana X. Bible had just wound up his remarkable career at the University of Texas. If I may steal a line from Darrell Royal, these guys didn't come to town on a load of wood. There were no soft touches.

One week before we were' to open the 1947 season against Stephen F. Austin we had the boosters, the Bear Club members, come in from all over the state to see their new coach operate. We had a formal scrimmage, the varsity vs. the B team. The B team beat us 7-0. I thought we'd be fired on the spot, but Woodruff was delighted. "Boy, that's the best thing that could ever happen to us," he said. "Now we'll be ready." I didn't know what he was talking about at the time, but he was saying our players would be worried, frustrated, and fired up. We won our first four games and finished 5-5 with rather meager material. Everybody was happy for the time being because Baylor had won only one game the year before. We knew we had to find a quarterback to build around if we were going to make steady progress. We opened up with Jack Price, a heady player and a good passer, but slow. Hayden Fry was there—in fact, Hayden was the first person I met on the Baylor campus—but he was just out of high school and not ready. I've often said that if we hadn't recruited Adrian Burk, I'd be selling insurance somewhere.

Adrian was a single wing back at Kilgore Junior College, which had played in the Little Rose Bowl—sort of an unofficial junior college national championship game. Adrian's Kilgore coach told us he thought he could be a great T-quarterback; he'd played some T-formation in high school. Adrian planned to go to TCU; in fact, his clothes were already there. This was in August of 1948, and Adrian had to go to a National Guard camp at Fort Hood for a couple of weeks. I was there to see him every afternoon at five o'clock. Buddy Attaway, the center off his team, was already at Baylor, and I took him with me to see Adrian every day. We'd go through all the quarterback maneuvers with him, and I could see he'd be great. He picked up everything instantly.

We didn't have a signing date then and no binding letter of intent. You fought for athletes until they enrolled in school—and often after that. There were lots of "grid-napping" cases in those days, and few schools were blameless. Anyway, I thought we'd sold Adrian on coming with us, but when he left the Guard camp, he just disappeared. TCU couldn't find him, and we didn't have any idea where he was. We finally located him about three days later at Shreveport, where his girl friend lived. He was staying with her family trying to decide what he should do. He'd been so worried and upset he couldn't even eat. We went and got him, brought him to Waco, bought him a steak, and he said he'd enroll at Baylor. We wrote to TCU to try to get his clothes back.

For every successful recruiting yarn, though, you wind up on the wrong end of a dozen others. We thought we had Bud McFadin, one of the all-time SWC linemen, All-American tackle at Texas, and later a tremendous pro. We put him in a Baylor uniform about August 20 and took photos for publicity releases. I vividly remember going out and visiting with him at Iraan, Texas, where his dad was a tenant on a big ranching and farming spread. Bud came out to greet me in blue jeans with no shirt. I'd never seen a more physical-looking football player in my life.

Bud went to a high school All-Star game. Hayden Fry was in the game and he was watch-dogging McFadin for us. I was on the scene at all times, too. In fact, Bud and Hayden lived in my motel room because it was air-conditioned. They didn't want to stay in the dorm where the All-Star kids were quartered; it was too hot. We thought everything was fine. We went home and Bud went home, and when it came the day to report he didn't show up at Baylor. Woodruff and I were frantic. We got Hayden to call some of his high school buddies at SMU, and Bud wasn't there. He checked a friend at TCU, and Bud wasn't there. He finally called one of the players at Texas and said, "Hey, have you seen ol' Bud McFadin since the All-Star game?" "Sure," the kid said, "He's in school here."

I took Hayden and we drove to Austin. Hayden went into the dormitory and talked to Bud about 10 minutes. McFadin stayed at Texas, and I went home with a good lesson. When you've got one, or think you have, don't let him out of your sight. Above all, keep him away from your opponents. That was the law of the jungle, you might say. Things are so much better now, with the national letter of intent, and a uniform NCAA code on recruiting (not perfect, but better).

Waco represents a hectic, happy, coming-of-age period for Barbara and me. I was making $300 a month, which seemed like a lot of money in 1947. We paid $6700 for a little frame house on 24th Street. Jack and Hank, our first two sons, were born during our Baylor hitch. George Berry Graves and his wife Louise, fervent Baylor boosters, sort of took us under their wings like a father and mother. He's a top Baylor Bear Club member to this day, but, although we root in different directions in the Southwest Conference, we're personally as close as ever.

Soon after we arrived, Bob Woodruff sent me to Bay City, Texas, to make a speech. I was just out of college, and I didn't know a thing about speaking in public. High school kids can get up and express themselves like pros nowadays, but it was a new experience for me and I was scared. During this trip, driving down the highway and worrying, I made a commitment that my life would reflect the same virtues that I was teaching on the football field. I thought that was the purpose for me being in coaching rather than baseball, which I'd wanted to be, and I accepted it. On that particular trip, I felt a real closeness to Jesus Christ. I made some commitments there about my life, my work, the relationship I hoped to have with my players, and the example I would try to set.

After our first season, Herman Hickman offered me an assistant's job at Yale for $7000 a year. I was flattered, but Woodruff said he'd give me a nice raise, so I turned Hickman down. Well, I waited and waited and waited for the raise, and then learned that Bill Henderson and Jim Cros were also making $300 a month. Henderson had been there since 1936, Crow since 1919. Money was tight in Waco in those days. To give me a raise, Woodruff obviously had to give these fine gentlemen a raise, too. Finally, he gave all three of us $600 raises to $4200 a year.

Our program was climbing. We had a 5-3-2 record in '48 and beat Wake Forest in the Dixie Bowl at Birmingham. The Baptist Bowl, everybody said, because Baylor and Wake Forest were the top Baptist colleges in the country. Adrian Burk was everything we thought he could be—and more. We nearly won it all in '49. We won our first five games, and lost only to Texas in our first nine.

When we beat SMU at Dallas, we just knew we were going to the Cotton Bowl. Baylor had never been. The Bears' last previous conference championship had been in 1924, and there was no Cotton Bowl then. As you probably know, they didn't make it until Grant Teaff's 1974 Bears ended a 50-year drouth. Baylor had a lot of agonizing near-misses over the years, and '49 turned out to be one of them. Anyway, the day we whipped SMU in a great game, 35-26, we considered ourselves unstoppable.

As crazy as it may sound, I dreamed a pass play for that game. I mean I actually saw it in a dream. I told Woodruff about the play, and it appealed to him. "We are not only going to use it," he said, "we're going to use it on the first play of the game." We practiced it all week. Woodruff told each of the starters, "Block your man, don't hold, don't get a penalty. We're going to score on the first play of the game." Have you ever acted out a dream? We got the ball on our 20 after the kickoff. Dudley Parker, the wingback, faked and then took off deep. Burk hit him for an 80-yard touchdown.

Matty Bell's Mustangs, with their talent and razzle-dazzle offense, were the top drawing card in the league in those days. Doak
Walker, Kyle Rote . . . magic names. Doak was the last of the three-
time All-American heroes, and if there was something he couldn't
do on a football field to beat you, nobody ever found it out. SMU
won the championship in '47 and '48, but in '49, with Doak a senior
and everybody gunning for them, they suffered through an injury-
plagued, up-and-down season. You never felt at ease against SMU;
they were so explosive. I was upstairs in the press box, calling the
plays, and with 30 seconds to go in the first half, we were leading by a
touchdown and SMU was lining up in punt formation. I had to get to
the dressing room, but as I hurried down the thought flashed
through my mind, "He won't kick." Walker, I meant. Just then, I
heard that sudden, engulfing roar from the crowd that means something major had happened. "Oh, my gosh," I said. "That Walker
faked a punt and scored!" I ran out of the elevator and grabbed the
first fan I could reach. "What happened?" I screamed.

"What happened?" he said. "Why, those blankety-blanks scored,
that's what happened."

"Which blankety-blanks?" I blurted. He shot me a disgusted look.
"Baylor," he said.

Walker had failed on a fake kick, and we took over in time for
Burk to throw to Stanley Williams for a touchdown before the half
ran out. I'll never forget that SMU fan.

Rice had what was no doubt Jess Neely's best team ever. Everything came down to the final week, Baylor vs. Rice, in the last game
ever played in the old Rice Stadium at Houston. If we won, we'd tie
Rice for the title and go to the Cotton Bowl. We were all fired up; we
were going to make Baylor history in our third year. You talk about a
letdown. We took the opening kick-off and picked them apart—
nothing big, just a good, steady drive—and went ahead 7-0. From
then on it was all Rice. They beat us convincingly 21-7.

Woodruff was much in demand as a head coaching candidate all
over the country, and I was beginning to be noticed as an assistant.
When Bernie Moore retired as LSU coach, that job was offered to
Bob. Baylor's Board members knew he wouldn't go without a release, so they wouldn't give him one. He called his best friend on the
athletic committee and told him about the LSU offer. "We'll let you

out of your contract," the committeeman said.

"Oh, I wouldn't leave if you didn't," Bob said. So they didn't and he stayed on.

LSU's head coaching job went to Gaynell Tinsley after Bob withdrew, and LSU offered me $8000 to go there as Tinsley's assistant. Woodruff was in Houston at the Shamrock Hotel, and I couldn't get in touch with him. I hopped the next plane to Houston to tell Bob I was leaving, and I arrived about 10 o'clock on a Saturday night. I was going to fly on to Baton Rouge early the next morning. I couldn't reach him that night, so I phoned his room about daybreak. I told him I was going to LSU for $8000 a year.

He sounded very calm and cheerful. "Frank, have you looked outside? No? Well, look outside."

You know it never snows in Houston, except this time it did. The biggest snowstorm in 25 years was outside my window. Planes were grounded. I had to stay there with him all day, and by noon he'd talked me out of it. He got me raised up to $5400, and I was satisfied. Bob could talk me into anything.

A few day after our loss to Rice in '49, I was running around Houston recruiting, bragging about Baylor's 8-2 record, when I picked up a paper and read that Woodruff had a run-in with Baylor athletic director Raymond "Bear" Wolf. Woodruff said if he couldn't control his football program, he'd be resigning. This had been simmering in the background a long while, and when it came out in the open, everybody instantly took sides. Finally, it seemed they resolved their differences, and Bob said he'd stay. During the Christmas holidays, Bob called me. "Frank, I'm going to take the Florida job," he said. "Athletic director, everything. Don't tell a soul. I want you to sit tight there, and I'll bring you to Florida after I've taken the job."

Bob went to Florida for about $17,000 a year when most major head coaches were making $10,000 to $12,000. I don't know why he wanted me to stay at Baylor, but I said I would. I had to take the brunt of him pulling out. People were calling him every name in the book, and I had to stand in for him on the ground-breaking ceremony for the new Baylor stadium, for which we'd campaigned hard. I've got $80 of my money in the Baylor stadium. I stayed there about a month among those upset and indignant people. Some of my friends wanted me to apply for the Baylor job. They thought I was 28, but I was actually 25 and I knew I wasn't ready to be a head coach.

"The Korean War broke out as we were establishing our staff at Florida."
Courtesy of Georgia Tech Athletic Association

I went on to Florida for $7200. Sometimes, dealing with Woodruff was like pulling eye teeth.

My year at Florida was one of the few times I've really been un-happy in coaching. Bob had four coaches, and he put me in charge of the defensive backs. I'd coached both offense and defense at Baylor and called the plays, so this was a demotion and a blow to my pride. Bob explained it had to be that way on an expanded staff with two-platoon football in full flower.

The Korean War broke out as we were establishing our staff at Florida. All through the summer of 1950, everybody pondered their military status. Not ol' Frank, though. "I'm in the Naval Reserve," I said off-handedly one day. "I've never attended a meeting. They don't want me. If they do, I guess they know where to find me."

A couple of days later on a Saturday morning I was going through my mail at the office. I pulled out an official envelope: Navy Department. Inside was a list of things they might want you to do, and one category was checked: "Get your personal business in order and report in 30 days for active duty." Maybe the wording was more formal, but that was the message. I turned white as a sheet. I went into shock. I went running into Woodruff's office where all the coaches were sitting around drinking coffee and gabbing. "Look at this!"

"Well, Frank," Woodruff said, "I thought you were through with the Navy. They didn't want you."

Everybody snickered a little.

I called Barbara, and naturally it shook her up. I paced the floor about 30 minutes until the secretary called me to the phone. It was Barbara. Somebody had been kind enough to call her and tell her it was a joke. They had borrowed someone else's form and fixed it up for me. I went rushing back, and all the coaches were rolling around on the floor laughing. I felt angry, foolish, and happy all at the same time. They'd really nailed me.

During the latter part of the summer, some of the Georgia Tech assistant coaches went fishing in Florida, and they came to Gainesville and told me Bobby Dodd was going to enlarge and reorganize his staff in December. Would I be interested? Well, I was unhappy. I took the position that I would definitely be interested in talking about it.

We had a sophomore team at Florida and a 5-5 record in '50 (Doug Dickey was a freshman quarterback). Alabama was the best team we played by far. They ran the split-T and mixed it with the Notre Dame box, and we couldn't stop them. Woodruff decided to play 12 men against them. He didn't think anybody would notice it. We were playing a 6-3-2, and as Alabama moved close to our goal line we slipped the extra man in, and we were in a 6-3-2-1. We still didn't stop them, and about the third time we tried it they caught it and penalized us 15 yards.

As soon as the season was over, Ray Graves called me from Tech. "Yeah, I'm still interested," I said. I talked to Woodruff about it, and he didn't want me to go. He said I could switch to offense, and all the problems could be worked out. As I've said, Bob could convince me of anything. I told him I'd stay, and I called Dodd and asked him to withdraw my name from consideration. Fine, Dodd said. A couple of hours later, he called me back. "Frank, I tried to explain your feelings to some of the Regents and the athletic committee people but they can't understand why you, an alumnus and all, wouldn't want to come back. Their feelings are hurt. Would you mind coming up and talking to them?"

I said I'd be happy to come, and I called and made my reservations. I knew if I went to Atlanta, I might take the job, so I went over and cleaned out my desk. All my playbooks, my Baylor notes, my Florida notes, everything. I took them home and stacked them in a big cardboard box.

After I visited Tech and talked with everybody, I was certain I wanted to go back there. I called Woodruff, and he was really upset.

"You promised you wouldn't decide up there," he said.

"Bob, I knew if I came back, you'd talk me out of it," I said. "And this is definitely what I want to do."

When I reached home, Barbara was in tears. She told me Bob had come over and demanded to know where those notebooks were. He had sent another assistant coach, Hobe Hooser, to clean out my desk, and discovered I had beat him to the punch. Bob just walked into our house, found them, and took them with him.

By the time I reached Bob's office, I was in a conciliatory frame of mind. I wanted my notebooks. When I walked in, he just looked at me and handed me a letter. "Read this before you say anything," he said. He'd written something like this: "Dear Frank: We appreciate all you have contributed to our staff and organization. You have been paid for it. Everything you've done, all your playbooks and notebooks, belongs to this organization instead of you. I hope you understand that."

I handed the note back to him. "Bob, you can't mean that."

"The hell I don't," he said.

"Just let me make copies of everything," I said. "I need my notes. The things I've put together the last four years are priceless to me."

"Nope," he said. "They stay with this organization."

I kept saying I had to have those things. He finally said he'd think about it. He called me in the next day and gave me copies of everything except my Florida notes. "Florida and Georgia Tech play each other," he reminded me. Basically, Bob and I were close friends (and still are), although reading some of this could give you cause to wonder. Woodruff wanted the edge, and he was an excellent football coach—a first-rate defensive coach and just extremely intelligent. All the way through our association, we argued and had our day-to-day differences over strategy. He was an old line coach, and he had his hunches. I'd call a play, and he'd "hunch" me right out of it, you know.

Here's the bottom line, though. He had faith in me, and gave me a responsible coaching position when I was 22 years old. I'd always be grateful to him, even if I didn't love him, which I do.

7
THE BOWLING HABIT

It was 1952, and the Georgia Tech Yellowjackets were playing on a muddy field in Athens, trying to nail down their first perfect football season in 24 years. Except for a wartime game the University of Georgia always discounted, Tech hadn't beaten Georgia in Athens since the 1920s. We were losing 7-3 in the third quarter. Bobby Dodd, who ordinarily stood calmly and patiently in one spot on the sidelines, was pacing up and down like any other coach that day. We worked the ball down to the Georgia 10, where we had fourth and three. Dodd called time out and said to me, "I want to throw the belly pass . . . back to the short side."

"Coach Dodd, we haven't practiced it this year," I blurted out.

"I don't care," Dodd said. He looked up and down the bench and called Chappell Rhino, a third-string halfback who didn't play anymore. He'd lost his speed after he suffered a broken ankle playing semi-pro baseball for my old Dixie Steel team. I'd been on the Tech staff two years at this time, and I'd never seen Chappell Rhino throw a pass even in practice. Dodd sort of casually put his arm around Rhino's shoulders. "Chappell, we're gonna throw the belly pass," he said. "Here's what I want you to do. Go in there and tell (quarterback) Bill Brigman to call the belly. If the cornerback lays back, you run for the first down. If he takes the fake and comes up, you just throw it over his head to Buck Martin."

Rhino started to protest that he hadn't worked on it. Dodd just smiled and nudged him toward the field. "He can do it," he said to me.

I couldn't bear to look. I turned the other way. I had to see it on film later. We lined up in left formation, and Georgia moved its de-

Bobby Dodd and his staff; left to right: Standing—Jack Griffin, Lewis Woodruff, Whitey Urban, and Trainer Buck Andel. Kneeling—Ray Graves, Bobby Dodd, Frank Broyles, and Tonto Coleman.

fense. We started back to the right. We faked and pitched to Rhino. The defensive back came charging across the line of scrimmage. Rhino floated the ball to Martin in the end zone. We went ahead, 10-7, and eventually won, 23-9.

Bobby Dodd was the first "modern" head football coach, the only one of his time who could really delegate responsibility. He called me in when he hired me in 1951, and this is all he said: "Frank, you're gonna coach the offense. You head it up. I'll watch and if I see some things I don't like, I'll call you in. Don't come running to me with everything. You work it out. I don't want to see you in this office. If something's wrong, I'll be in your office."

He gave the defense to Ray Graves, and told him essentially the same thing. We weren't supposed to go to him and ask a question. He met with us when he didn't like what we were doing and changed things. Everybody tries to coach like that now, I guess. Almost everybody. The "chairman of the board" approach.

On Fridays, he really warmed up, got involved. He'd quiz the quarterback and everybody else, and he'd take charge and we'd play some kind of a joke game up and down the field—just loosen up, laugh, have fun.

During my six years on Dodd's staff, 1951-56, Tech had regular-season records of 10-0-1, 11-0, 8-2-1, 7-3, 8-1-1, and 9-1, and followed up by winning a bowl game each time. We beat Baylor in the Orange 17-14; Mississippi in the Sugar 24-7; West Virginia in the Sugar 42-19; Arkansas in the Cotton 14-6; Pittsburgh in the Sugar 7-0, and Pitt again in the Gator 21-14. Dodd's relaxed approach to bowl games was widely scorned at first, but eventually copied. How could you argue with success?

"Nobody else can coach like Dodd and win," Paul "Bear" Bryant said during the 1950s, but over the years, Coach Bryant adopted much of Dodd's approach. They all did.

Dodd had been a University of Tennessee quarterback, and he absorbed all the Tennessee precepts of General Bob Neyland (soundness, defense, kicking), but he refined them with flexibility and flair. He shortened his practices. He usually eliminated contact work by the time the schedule started. He preached positive thinking. All these things are taken for granted now, but we're talking about 25-30 years ago.

The belly series became our complete offense. It wasn't just one play or a fake off one play; we could attack all the way across the board with it. The inside belly and outside belly, as devised by Georgia Tech, became the rage of college football by the middle 1950s, and the inside belly off-tackle run remains the number one goal-line play in football, no matter which formation is used.

We happened upon it almost by accident. Eddie LeBaron, a fine little pro quarterback later, discovered the basic elements of it while he was playing for College of the Pacific. Dodd and LeBaron were together in the summer of 1950 while Dodd worked with the College All-Star squad at Chicago. Tech used it some in '50 without success, and we kept tinkering with it in '51. Our breakthrough came late in the season. We beat Alabama in a rugged game, 27-7, and we had a play with the guard pulling and trapping the end out, the dive back filling for the guard, and the fullback running off tackle. Alabama played a 6-2 defense, and, when they'd see this develop, their end would close and just destroy the offensive guard and close the hole.

While I was looking at the film, I thought of all Dodd's talk about the belly series, and I envisioned the same play—except that when the guard pulled and the end closed, the quarterback would pull back the ball and pitch it out instead. I told Ray Graves about it, and he liked it. Our Georgia game loomed, and Georgia played the same defense as Alabama. Before practice the next day, I ran through it with our senior quarterback, Darrell Crawford. On the practice field, I said, "Coach Dodd, I'd like for you to line up at end and try to defense this play we've got." We were, of course, just moving through it without contact.

"Sure," Dodd said. He didn't know if we were kidding or not, but he stepped in to be the defensive end.

We started the off-tackle play, and, when the guard pulled, Dodd stepped inside him to meet the fullback. Crawford faked the hand-off, "rode" with the fullback just long enough, and pitched out. Everybody laughed, and Dodd was impressed. We put in the play for Georgia.

In a 48-6 victory, we scored five touchdowns off the belly series. The first time we ran it, Leon Hardeman went 40 yards for a touchdown, and the first man who knew he had the ball and stood a chance to make the play was the off-side defensive halfback. The safety, the cornerback, the linebacker, and the defensive end all took the fullback fake inside. We ran it away from the defensive right halfback, and he dashed all the way across the field and had a shot at Hardeman around the five.

We had fine backs (Hardeman, Glen Turner, Billy Teas) running an innovative new offense that picked up fresh wrinkles by the week. We had a tremendous offensive line that was large (230-235 pounds per man) for that day and age. Our defensive players were quick, swarming kids under the direction of a master defensive coach, Ray Graves. We didn't lose for two and a half years until Notre Dame beat us in '53. Tech went undefeated in 31 consecutive games with two ties.

Dodd was a marvel with the players, the assistants, the press, the fans, the alumni, the Atlanta business community. Dodd possessed the warmth, charm, and intellect to have been anything on earth he wanted to be. He didn't have a lot of rules, but he was firm as a rock when it was necessary to discipline players. Essentially he insisted that they go to class, go to church, and stay out of trouble. There never was a better coach on the sidelines. When he had a hunch, as in the Chappell Rhino incident, he never hesitated, never looked back. He had an instinct for knowing when a daring, unexpected move would lift his team and shatter the opponent—and when it would have the reverse effect. He made some great, great calls. During a game, about all he'd say to me was, "Frank, we're not throwing enough," or "Frank, we've got to run more up the middle."

Dodd impressed on me two things more than anything else: (1) Practice and playing are different, and some players are "game" players. (2) Some of your best players don't necessarily look like great athletes. Pepper Rodgers, a quarterback with no special ability except to win, was the central example for both lessons.

When we were getting ready for our first game in '51 against SMU, we knew we had the makings of an exceptional football team—except that we didn't have a place kicker. I was working with two of them, Glen Turner and Pepper Rodgers. Turner, our regular fullback, kicked those beautiful line-drive extra points. BOOM! Prettiest thing you've ever seen. Pepper took a little short step and just barely blooped the ball up there.

"Well, Frank who do you think should kick?" Dodd asked me on Friday.

"Turner," I said. "Turner. No question. Turner."

He walked over toward Turner, and motioned that I should follow him.

"Glen, son, you've done well kicking," he said. "Would you like to kick against SMU?"

"Coach, I'll do the best I can," he said. "You know that."

Dodd walked over to Pepper Rodgers.

"Pepper, you've been doing pretty well kicking. How'd you like to kick tomorrow?"

"Coach, how many people are gonna be here?" Pepper asked.

Dodd told him they were expecting a crowd of 40,000.

"Then I'll never miss," Pepper said. "Not with 40,000 people looking at me."

He kicked 35 extra points in a row. He handled our place-kicking his whole career at Georgia Tech. Turner never kicked a one. I can still see Pepper in the Orange Bowl against Baylor jumping and raising his hands, signalling that his field goal was good before the officials did. That field goal beat Baylor 17-14. The score was 14-14 and it was hot, and the game had slowed to a walk before Pepper won it.

The most we ever practiced for a bowl game was three days—at the bowl site, I mean. Dodd figured if you practiced more than that, the players would get sore and then you had to practice three or four times to work out the soreness. You'd leave your game on the practice field. We worked hard, but he made the players think we didn't. They were having a good time. He convinced the squad they'd play well because they'd be fresh. The day after, they'd be too sore to walk, but they didn't have to play again until spring practice. He won six straight bowl games with this theory.

We were 11-0 in '52, number two to Michigan State in the polls, and Dodd wanted to make a second straight trip to the Orange Bowl. We also had a Sugar Bowl bid. We called a squad meeting.

"Okay, how many want to go back to the Orange Bowl?" Dodd asked. "You remember—beaches, pretty girls, sunshine." The squad registered a near-unanimous vote for the Orange.

I sensed that a lot of them weren't too keen about it, but they weren't going to vote against Dodd. About that time, the ol' Decatur redhead opened his big mouth.

"Coach Dodd, would you mind if I talked to 'em, and we took another vote?" I asked.

"Sure, go ahead," Dodd said.

I got up and made an impassioned pitch for the Sugar Bowl. New places, new friends. Spread it around. We've been to the Orange Bowl. They held another vote. It was practically unanimous for the Sugar Bowl. Dodd didn't say anything, but he didn't like it. He accepted the Sugar Bowl bid.

This was when you could accept two or three weeks before your season was over. The Sugar Bowl matched us with Ole Miss, a conference opponent we hadn't played during the season. We didn't have a full round robin in the Southeastern Conference, and Tech and Ole Miss avoided each other because of some lingering argument about something or other. Dates and sites probably. They didn't care to come to Atlanta, and we didn't care to go to Oxford. Anyway, Dodd was upset.

"I can't believe I let you talk me into this," he said to me.

I didn't say a word.

The Orange Bowl picked Syracuse, which was just beginning to move up a little, but was nowhere near the peak it would hit a few years later with Jimmy Brown and the great players who came after Brown. Since they couldn't get Tech, the Orange Bowl people picked Alabama as Syracuse's opponent.

"I don't believe this," Dodd said. "We could be in Miami playing Syracuse, and we're going to New Orleans to play Mississippi."

I didn't open my mouth.

We were going to be in New Orleans three days before the game. It rained; the weather was miserable. We were on a bus going to practice in the rain, and some of the players showed me a newspaper clipping of Alabama players on the beach with their arms around pretty girls who were smiling and holding oranges. Our players passed that paper all over the bus, and when they weren't looking at it they were staring out the window at the rain. I wanted to crawl under a seat.

Mississippi got the opening kick-off and took it right in and scored. We were behind, 7-0, when the PA announcer said Alabama was leading Syracuse 31-0 after one quarter. I was upstairs, calling the offense from the press box. Dodd got me on the phone. "Do you realize what you've done? Did you hear that score?"

"Yes sir," I said.

Mississippi drove to our one-yard line, had a couple of shots at it, and didn't score. Except that Ole Miss coach Johnny Vaught, the Mississippi governor, and everybody else in the state swore they went in.

Ray Graves then made a vital defensive adjustment. We left our 5-4 and went to a split six with two linebackers firing up the middle. We had used it on rare occasions, and it was perfect for this occasion. Ole Miss stopped dead in its tracks, and our belly series started taking us down the field again and again. We won going away 24-7.

Afterward, Ole Miss coaches took that game film all over Mississippi and yelled that three or four of the officials in the game were from Atlanta. Alabama beat Syracuse 61-6. We won the Sugar Bowl impressively, but we had to listen to Mississippi flak for months.

The next four years, we made two more trips to the Sugar Bowl, one to the Cotton, and to the Gator. Dodd presented the bids, and the players voted. They received no advice from Frank Broyles—and asked none.

8
DUCKS ON THE POND

Georgia Tech and Arkansas played the 1955 Cotton Bowl game against a background of speculation that Bowden Wyatt, the Arkansas coach, would soon depart for his alma mater, the University of Tennessee. At a party the bowl people threw for both coaching staffs, I lingered a while after shaking hands with Arkansas athletic director John Barnhill. "Barnie, I've heard all the rumors," I said. "I hope you can keep Bowden, but if you don't, I really want you to consider me for the job."

"Why do you want to be a head coach?" Barnie asked. "You should be happy where you are. You and Bobby got it made. A bowl every year...."

Mrs. Barnhill, who was listening, smiled at me. "You should never want to be a head coach, Frank. You've got the best of all worlds now."

That was the prevailing view from a distance, and, because of it, I despaired of ever getting a chance as a head coach. Wyatt left Arkansas, and Jack Mitchell was selected to replace him. I didn't even get an interview.

I wasn't so restless the first couple of years on the Tech staff. I was young, I knew I wasn't ready to be a head coach, I knew I had much to learn. Then, as I neared 30 and saw people in my age bracket moving ahead of me (Darrell Royal, Paul Dietzel, Jack Mitchell), I felt I was on a treadmill. My situation at Tech was touchy and complicated from the beginning. In the spring of '51, Bobby Dodd enlarged his staff to three offensive coaches and three defensive coaches—really a giant step forward in the structural part of a modern football staff. Dodd put me in charge of offense and Ray Graves in charge of defense. Ray Ellis and Dwight Keith were still there. Both were good friends of mine. Ellis had been my backfield coach when I was a player, and that was one of the reasons I hesitated about the job; I wasn't sure everything would work out. They assured me the situation would resolve itself, and it did. Dwight was ready to retire and run his *Scholastic Coach* magazine, and Ellis soon resigned and left coaching.

Often, it's a mistake to go back home and try to work among the people who knew you when you were coming up. Your old friends have some kind of a role mapped out for you in their minds. I'd been back in Atlanta a couple of months when I realized some people thought I would be the freshman coach rather than the offensive coach. I'd played there only four years before, and some figured I was too green for any top responsibility. Dodd told me there was no question in his mind, but the public debate about my status really deflated my ego. Although he was in his 40s and at the peak of his career, Dodd talked of retiring all the time. I never took that seriously, but a lot of people did. When we played Baylor in the Orange Bowl after the '51 season, one of the papers had a story that it would be Dodd's last game.

Just as there were some Tech fans who thought I should be freshman coach, others figured I was Dodd's successor, that I'd been brought back to Tech to be groomed. I knew Ray Graves deserved the job before I did. Ray was older and more experienced than I was, and he was close to Dodd. One of my friends told me he heard I had no chance of leaving Georgia Tech because no one there would give me a recommendation. I didn't believe that, but it upset me to know such rumors were in circulation. I was afraid I'd be trapped: Dodd would retire, and Graves might not keep me. I sweated three years, hoping Dodd wouldn't retire before I landed a head-coaching job.

I don't know if Graves believed me or not, but I told him he was the natural choice as Dodd's successor and that I didn't want the Georgia Tech job. People far removed from the scene were telling each other: "Broyles won't ever leave Georgia Tech. He's Dodd's replacement." I was crying to leave, begging to leave. Vanderbilt people talked to me through Fred Russell, the *Nashville Banner* sports editor, but at the last minute Vanderbilt switched to Art Guepe, who'd been head coach at the University of Virginia. I never had official contact from the school.

In fact, all through this period, I formally interviewed for only one job. I had a very good meeting with board members of the University of Houston, and they made a kind of gentleman's agreement they would offer me the job. I put them off until after the Cotton Bowl game against Arkansas, and when we got the game out of the way I discussed the offer with Dodd. He advised me not to take it. Houston was in the Missouri Valley Conference then, and about to go independent. Houston was struggling to make it as a big-time team in a city long dominated by Rice University. Dodd said I should wait for a better-established job to open. I'd concluded that myself, but the conversation gave me an opening to say a few other things.

"Coach, it's tough for me to get a job," I said. "Most people won't call you because they know I'm a Georgia Tech man and I'm probably gonna stay here. Ray (Graves) wants to be a head coach just as much as I do. Would you do this? If a job comes open and Ray wants it, recommend him and don't recommend me. If I want a job, then recommend me. We cancel each other out when we're in the running for the same job. Two recommendations are worse than none."

"That makes sense," Dodd said. "I'll help both of you as much as I can."

A few days later, Gaynell Tinsley was released by LSU, and one of the best jobs in the Southeastern Conference opened. Appeared to open, that is. Actually, Paul Dietzel held the inside track all the way, but the school elected to go through a coach-hunting ritual. I went to Dodd. "If Ray is interested in the LSU job, I won't be," I said. "But if he's not, would you recommend me?" He said he would. A couple of days later, a speculation list of the LSU candidates appeared in the paper. Both Graves and Broyles were mentioned as possibilities. Dodd didn't have anything to do with it—some writer was trying to cover all possibilities—but that article really destroyed me. I felt I'd never land a good coaching job then.

December and January were terrible months for me. Each winter I got my hopes up over this or that vacancy, and when it closed, I felt despondent, frustrated, miserable. On the field, things couldn't have been better. Dodd was a great man to work for and a great man to learn from. He was so far ahead of his time it was unreal. Offense, defense, strategy, organization, public relations: most procedures coaches take for granted today can be traced back to Bobby Dodd. Also, he had a great love for the players and he put the classroom ahead of the stadium; not many coaches at that time were prepared to do that. Observing Dodd gave you the background to put things in perspective, get first things first.

Including bowl games, we went 61-7-2 in my six years on the Tech staff. We had 10 All-Americans to work with: Lamar Wheat, Ray Beck, Buck Martin, Harold Miller, George Morris, Pete Brown, Robert Moorhead, Leon Hardeman, Larry Morris, and Don Stephenson. We won in the plush two-platoon times, and we adjusted and kept winning (though not at the same rate) after free substitution was banned in 1953, and college football reverted to pre-war restrictions on the use of players. We grew more conservative with the change and stressed the kicking game and defense. To beat Georgia Tech in Grant Field "with their officials" was tough duty, our opponents said. Many of the SEC officials lived in Atlanta where the league headquarters were located.

In 1956, we figured we'd have our best team since we went 22-0-1 in 1951-52. However, '56 was Bowden Wyatt's 10-0 year at Tennessee, and Tech lost only to Tennessee, 6-0. The Tech-Tennessee game grew into the greatest showdown ever played in Atlanta to that time, and you couldn't believe the interest, the tension. Tennessee and Georgia Tech were right up there with Oklahoma for No. 1 in the nation, and tickets could be scalped for $100 to $150 apiece. Two or three thousand people tore down a fence and came in to see the game.

We couldn't get going. Tennessee played a wide-tackle-six, unlike any other defense we saw during the year, and we couldn't block it. We didn't move, but they weren't doing much either, and we went to the half 0-0. Johnny Majors, Tennessee's senior All-American tailback (and, of course, the same Johnny Majors of later coaching fame) was a terrific quick kicker. We backed up Tennessee to its five-yard line and alerted our safety to loosen up for a quick kick. Majors ran off tackle a couple of times and made a first down. We brought our safety up a little bit, and Majors delivered the most outlandish quick kick I've ever seen in my life.

The ball rolled 75 yards, and really put us in the hole. We punted out, and they came back with the first pass they'd tried all day, a little out pattern to Buddy Cruze, their weakside end and a heck of a player. Cruze caught about a 10-yarder. On the next down, Cruze ran another short route. Our quarterback, Wade Mitchell, was also a fine safety, but he'd hurt his shoulder and missed the first three games. He still favored the shoulder. To show you how things work sometimes, all he had to do was step in and make the tackle for a nominal gain, but he turned to hit with his good shoulder, and somebody had time to block him. Cruze ran to our five, and Tennessee punched it in for a touchdown.

After the season ended, I went to Dodd and told him what I'd been turning over in my mind for months. "I'm leaving Georgia Tech," I said, "even if I don't get a head job. I've done all I can do here, and I think I'd be hurting you to stay any longer. If necessary, I'll take another assistant's job somewhere. Maybe it would help me if I could catch on with Bud Wilkinson (Oklahoma) or Bear Bryant (then at Texas A&M). I'm asking you to help me get another job because this is the only way I can ever be a head coach."

"Well, I'll certainly help you," he said.

Don Faurot, one of the real gentleman coaches in the business, was retiring at the University of Missouri. The year before he'd talked to me about coming in as his backfield coach for the '56 season and then moving up to head coach. I couldn't consider that; you're never assured of anything in an arrangement of this type. Faurot interviewed a lot of people all through December of '56, and finally he called and asked me to visit. He said he would recommend me for the job.

"I really need your help," I told Dodd. "If you'll call the people up there at Missouri, maybe I can become a head coach."

He made some calls. With Bobby Dodd and Don Faurot both in my corner, how could I miss? Actually, it wasn't that cut-and-dried. I learned later there were 40 applicants for the Missouri job, and 14 received some degree of consideration.

Don Faurot, I guess you'd say, was a coaches' coach. His reputation inside the profession was absolutely tops, both for his personal traits and his football contributions. Faurot originated the split-T formation, which hit college football in the 1940s with the same impact the wishbone did in the late 1960s.

In 1941, Faurot had just lost his outstanding passer, Paul Christman, and was looking for an offense to generate the strongest running attack possible. He studied the Chicago Bears' "tight" T, and modified it in several significant ways. Don didn't care for the tight alignment, so he "split" his line, leaving 12 inches between center and guard, two feet between guard and tackle, and a yard between tackle and end. The tight-T quarterback, such as I was at Georgia Tech, did most of his work in a small area—he never carried the ball except on a sneak or a busted play. Faurot designed an offense that used the quarterback as a runner. Split-T quarterbacks would "slide" down the line rather than deliver the tight hand-off. The option, which Faurot compared to the two-on-one break in basketball, placed extreme pressure on the defensive end. When the defense committed itself, the quarterback kept or pitched to a trailing back. That feature of the split-T, of course, found its way into every modern college football offense you can name.

Faurot's 1941 team rushed for 307 yards per game, or nearly six yards per play. The top three rushers in the Big Six Conference that year were Missouri backs. Taken in the context of the times, these were sensational statistics.

During the war, Faurot served in the Navy with two young up-and-coming coaches named Jim Tatum and Bud Wilkinson. They installed Faurot's split-T at Oklahoma in 1946. After one year, Tatum left for Maryland to build a dynasty, and Wilkinson stayed at Oklahoma to crush the Big Eight with the split-T for years and years. Faurot never beat either of his pupils. The irony of it all was magnified by Maryland's 74-13 victory over Missouri in 1954.

Faurot was an idealist about recruiting. He came up with the Faurot Plan, or Missouri Plan, in which he limited his recruiting to the home state. He hoped it would catch on all across college football, but it didn't.

I wanted the job. I took the approach I could coach and win on that Missouri Plan. I accepted that principle, although at Georgia Tech we'd recruited all across the South—and anywhere else we could. The interview seemed to go well. I went back to the hotel and told Barbara, "I'm afraid to get my hopes up, but I believe we've got a chance." About that time, one of the board members called and said some of them would like to come and get me. They took me to dinner and told me they were offering me the job. I was officially hired the next day, although Missouri waited another couple of days to announce it at the NCAA coaches' convention at St. Louis.

I had one small second of doubt. As I waited outside the hotel for the board members, I realized it was cold in Columbia, Missouri. I stood there shivering, and I thought, "What's an ole Georgia boy doing here?"

"Barbara with Jack, Hank and friend."

I was 32 years old. At some point during my stay on the Tech staff, my actual age caught up with my "brochure" age. Barbara and I had four boys. Our first two sons, Jack and Hank, were born before we left Waco; Dan and Tommy were born in Atlanta.

As my first step toward establishing a Missouri staff, I hired Jerry Claiborne as my top defensive coach. Claiborne came from Bear Bryant at Texas A&M. For offense, I hired Merrill Green from Oklahoma. The characteristic Broyles luck surfaced again when Claiborne offered a recommendation. He asked me to consider adding a young coach named Jim Mackenzie, who was working at Allen Academy, a military junior college in Texas. I remembered Mackenzie from the 1952 All-Star game at Chicago. I was there helping Dodd with the College All-Stars, and Mackenzie had been one of Bryant's quality players at Kentucky.

The 1957 Missouri squad included some good linemen, but no backfield speed. We concluded we'd have to play it close to the vest, Tennessee style, and wait for the breaks. We quick-kicked a lot. Lo and behold, after seven games we were 5-1-1, 3-0 in the Big Eight, and locked up in an Orange Bowl showdown with Oklahoma.

In our opening game, we got away with a 7-7 tie with Vanderbilt when our center-linebacker Tom Swaney returned a pass interception for a touchdown. We beat Arizona, 35-13. Texas A&M came to Columbia with the No. 1 team in the country. The John David Crow Aggies were on a 12-game unbeaten streak, and I'll never forget chatting with Bear Bryant at midfield during the warmups. "Frank, I don't see a single damn athlete on your end of the field," Bear said. He wasn't being sarcastic; he was making a casual, matter-of-fact observation. They beat us, 28-0.

Our fans started getting excited when we squeaked past SMU, 7-6, and upset Colorado at Boulder, 9-6. That led us up to Oklahoma, which was on a 46-game winning streak and which had never lost a Big Eight game in Bud Wilkinson's tenure. Football forecasters all over the country made a Missouri upset of Oklahoma their "blue plate special" (remember those?) of the week. A lot of writers had been hinting for several weeks that the Sooners were ready to be taken. Missouri students held pep rallies every night. We were set up for the kill, and there was nothing we could do about it. In addition to their considerable physical tools, the Sooners had been handed the underdog's incentive. We stayed with them nearly three quarters and then our sophomore passer, Phil Snowden, was hurt, and they swamped us at the end, 39-14.

The next week, Notre Dame ended Oklahoma's 47-game winning streak with a 7-0 victory at Norman. Without Snowden, we

"Trying to find my directions at Missouri."

dropped our last two games to Kansas State and Kansas on field goals at the finish, 23-21 and 9-7. The week we played Kansas, rumors broke out that Jack Mitchell was certain to leave Arkansas and take the job at Kansas. "You don't think that's possible, do you?" I asked Don Faurot on the train ride to our Kansas game. "Kansas couldn't get Mitchell away from Arkansas, could they?"

"Frank, they got a seven-foot basketball player out of Philadelphia," Faurot said, referring to the recruitment of Wilt Chamberlain a couple of years earlier. "You know they can get a football coach out of Arkansas."

When Mitchell resigned a few days later to go to Kansas (his home-state University), I was dismayed to read that Murray Warmath of Minnesota was his probable replacement at Arkansas. "You think Barnie will even call me?" I asked Barbara every day. I suffered for nearly two weeks, reading about Murray Warmath and wondering. Then on a Saturday night I was home, and the telephone rang.

"Frank, this is Barnie."

"Barnie! What in the world took you so long?"

I meant the past two weeks, but in a way, I was talking about the past eight years.

Barnie laughed. "Well, do you want the job?" he asked.

"Do I want the job? You know I want the job, Barnie. I've always wanted the job."

"Well, I'll tell you what. Gimme until Tuesday. I've got to get my ducks on the pond" (that was his expression for lining up support for me, clinching the appointment.) "I'll get back to you Tuesday."

People assume I left Missouri because of the Missouri Plan on recruiting. No, I went into the Missouri Plan with my eyes wide open. Some think losing three straight at the end left me discouraged and receptive to Barnie's offer. I was discouraged, all right, but that wasn't a decisive factor, either. The job I'd always wanted was suddenly open to me. It was as simple as that.

Several times during the season, I'd talked to Don Faurot about some things we needed to change at Missouri to give us a better chance to win. He went to the athletic committee in my behalf, but they laughed him off. When I left after one season, I'm sure it became easier to get their attention. The Missouri Plan was quickly and quietly forgotten after Dan Devine replaced me. The Missouri Plan allowed us to go into adjacent areas like East St. Louis, Illinois, and Kansas City, Kansas, and when I agreed to it, I expected to pick up 15 or so prospects every year in the St. Louis area, and another 15 around Kansas City. Instead, we found only four or five players in the metropolitan areas. I was disappointed with the lack of emphasis on high school football in Missouri at that time. If I had remained, the Missouri Plan would have been scrapped, as it was for Devine, but I didn't leave because of it. In fact, our recruiting at Missouri turned out better than we believed at the time. Thirteen players off our 1957 freshman team were seniors on Devine's 1960 Orange Bowl team.

Missouri fans charged that I "jumped" a three-year contract. I'm not sure how legally binding the agreement was; the Missouri legislature frowned on long-term contracts. I had a personal understanding with Faurot that I could leave when I wanted to—after one year, three, five, or whatever. Faurot never reproached me for leaving, and I'll always be grateful to him for taking a chance on me.

"Harry Truman said, 'If you can't take the heat, get out of the kitchen.' That applies to coaching also."

Tuesday following Barnie's call, Jim Mackenzie and I were recruiting in East St. Louis. I was scheduled to call Barnie at three that afternoon, and I was so much on edge I couldn't even talk to any of the prospects. Jim said, "Hey, why don't I just drop you in a movie until three o'clock?" So I sat in a movie house in East St. Louis until it was time to make the call.

John Barnhill never wasted words. "The job's yours," he said. "The ducks are on the pond. We'll announce it Saturday."

On Friday, I went to Fayetteville and met with the faculty athletic committee. I picked up the papers and they were full of stories that Murray Warmath was about to be appointed coach at Arkansas. Had I come to the right town? The next day, Saturday, December 7, 1957, at four in the afternoon, the U of A Board of Trustees announced the appointment of Frank Broyles.

Arkansas people, I discovered during the next few weeks and

months, were weary of football coaches "just passing through" on their way to ultimate goals. Bowden Wyatt left for Tennessee after two seasons; Jack Mitchell pulled out for Kansas after three. In light of that, plus my brief stay at Missouri, many fans guessed I was working my way back to Georgia Tech. Little did they know.

9
BARNIE

At the end of World War II, John Barnhill could have had his pick of the attractive coaching vacancies. As interim head coach of the University of Tennessee, he took the Vols to a four-year record of 32-5-2, including trips to the Sugar Bowl and Rose Bowl. When General Bob Neyland returned from active duty to reclaim his job, Barnie had no inclination to resume his role as Neyland's line coach and chief assistant. Barnie struck out on his own, and the University of Arkansas job appealed to him. He'd seen good Arkansas athletes all over the Southeastern Conference for years. Alabama's Don Hutson and Paul "Bear" Bryant and LSU's Ken Kavanaugh were three spectacular examples. And there were dozens more. Barnie knew he could persuade Arkansas athletes to stay home in the future.

It all sounds so simple and inevitable in the retelling. Starting in 1946, Barnie built a statewide organization of Razorback Clubs, chased off outside recruiters, upgraded and expanded the facilities, and set in motion the modern Razorback football program. Of course, there were lean seasons, setbacks, disappointments, and criticism, but Barnie always clung to his vision and pushed on.

His first Arkansas squad, the war veterans of '46, earned a trip to the Cotton Bowl making it easier for Barnie to push for the expansion of Razorback Stadium at Fayetteville, and the building of War Memorial Stadium at Little Rock. Bowden Wyatt's "25 Little Pigs" of 1954, the classic underdog team, took the state by storm with a totally unexpected climb to the Southwest Conference championship and a Cotton Bowl bid. They packed War Memorial Stadium and paved the way to a higher plateau.

"Barnie gave me a raise even though we went 4-6 my first year."

Multiple sclerosis forced Barnie off the sidelines after the 1949 season, but as athletic director, he continued as the program's indispensable planner, organizer, and guide. He could see five or 10 years ahead as clearly as most men can guess what might happen day after tomorrow. He was like a second father to me. He was in terrible pain the last 15 years of his life—the 15 that I spent with him—and he never complained. You'd ask, "How do you feel, Barnie?" and he'd just shrug. "Aw, sometimes I think it might be better to just die," he'd say, "but the alternatives are to work hard and try to live with it." A few months before his death in 1973, he said one day: "Frank, you're trying to win, and I'm trying to stay alive. They're both hard to do."

He always took care of me. During the dark days in 1958, while we were losing our first six games and I was so low my chin scraped the floor, Barnie always went out of his way to try to pick me up. I'd walk into his office in the mornings, and he'd say, "Frank, your team is playing good and they're getting better. You're doing a good job and don't get discouraged." He'd call Barbara. He'd just pick up the phone, maybe on a Monday night, and say, "Barbara, don't you let Frank get discouraged. Don't you get discouraged, and don't you let Frank." He'd call my parents, and tell them not to worry about anything. At the end of the year, he gave me a raise, a new contract, and a $150,000 life insurance policy.

He was a master psychologist of young people; he knew what football players were thinking at all times. He could spot situations that would cause players to have a low level of inspiration rather than a high one. After we lost our first two games in '58, we looked like a 0-10 team for sure. Our third game was the conference opener with TCU, which was on its way to the championship. Barnie made the trips with us the first two or three years, and I'll never forget what he said before that game. During the pre-game meal, several of our players went to the restroom to throw up. Barnie said: "Boy, you're gonna play the best game you've ever played in your life." Then to me: "When they're throwing up the pre-game meal, they're ready."

With five minutes to play we were ahead of the best team in the league, 7-6. We punted, and a TCU player fumbled the catch and we recovered, but the official closest to the play had his view blocked, and the Horned Frogs kept the ball. Jack Spikes broke a trap play for 40 yards and they beat us, 12-7, but Barnie had sensed what kind of a game it would be. So I'd always go in and talk to him and ask, "Barnie, what is my team thinking?" I wasn't just making conversation; I wanted to know.

When I'd ask for something, large or small, he'd say, "Frank, I've only got one set of criteria. Will this help us win?" I'd say yes, and he'd say, "Okay, we'll do it."

In the spring of 1963, I wanted to put carpet in the dressing room and dining hall, and enlarge and spruce up the training room a little bit. He didn't like it, but he went along. In the late summer, I dropped in to chat with him one day.

"Frank, I hate to tell you this," he said. "But you're gonna have a bad year."

"Barnie, we're picked to win the conference," I said. "We won three championships in a row, then we had a 9-1 season last year and missed by half a game. Nearly everybody's back. What do you mean?"

"Frank, if you make things too comfortable for your players, they get lazy, self-satisfied. You've got to make it tough on 'em. Why do you think I built that training room with one little table in it? I'll tell you why. So half your team couldn't be in there getting taped, getting worked on—they'd be out on the field practicing. That's the reason we've got that little hole-in-the-wall for a training room. I could have built a big one. Putting in four or five different whirlpools and expanding the training room is not gonna help you. You're gonna have a bad year." Well, we did. We went 5-5.

After our 1964 team beat Nebraska in the Cotton Bowl for an 11-0 record and several versions of the national championship, I couldn't wait to get back to Barnie and share with him the culmination of a goal he'd set for Arkansas 18 years before. I floated into his office on cloud nine, ready to be emotional about the pinnacle of success and so forth. "Frank," he said before I could speak, "you've just screwed up the best job in America."

"What do you mean?" I finally managed to ask. I was back on my heels, dumbfounded.

"Don't you know you never win all your ball games? Keep 'em hungry. Eight, nine wins a year—you've been perfect. Now that you've done it all, they're gonna expect you to do it all the time. You've ruined this job." I spent two or three minutes trying to think of something to say.

When the NCAA opened up the 11th regular-season game early in 1970, I immediately booked Stanford for a Little Rock opener that fall, California for a 1971 opener, and Southern Cal for 1972, '73 and '74. Barnie was on emeritus status then, but he still spent time at the office every day, and he was still as wise and alert as ever. "Well, you ruined a good coaching job," he told me when I returned home. "You got rabbit-eared, that's what you did. I can't believe it. They tell you your schedule's weak because you won big, and now you're gonna go out and take on the world."

Barnie believed you had to win your first three games to sustain interest and assure your ticket sales. Win your first three, split the last eight, and that's 7-4 and probably a bowl bid. Start fresh, finish strong. Barnie had a little motto he preached to me all the time:

"People remember what you did in November." That became a kind of battle cry with us over the years. We didn't lose a November game until 1963, and we went 47-5 against our November opponents (Texas A&M, Rice, SMU, and Texas Tech) through my first 13 seasons at Arkansas.

Barnie seldom went into detail about anything. He could get his point across with a couple of old Tennessee sayings and start you thinking in the right direction. I made plenty of mistakes, but I can't think of a single one that sprang from any bad advice on Barnie's part. All young coaches should be able to start with a man like Barnie to lean on. Unfortunately, he was one of a kind.

10
SUPERBLY STAFFED

The first thing I did after accepting the Arkansas job was to go looking for a great defensive coach, and I came up with Jim Mackenzie. The second thing was to search out an exciting new offense, and I came up with the Iowa-Delaware winged-T. Well, one out of two isn't too bad for a beginner.

Jerry Claiborne resigned from my Missouri staff, even before I landed the Arkansas job, and went to Alabama as Bear Bryant's assistant head coach. Jerry left early to set up the machinery at Alabama while Bear took the Texas Aggies to a Gator Bowl game against Tennessee. Jerry was my defensive coordinator, and finding a new one was my top priority. I approached Charles McClendon, who was with Paul Dietzel at LSU, and Mike Campbell, Darrell Royal's defensive coach at Texas. They weren't interested. Finally I turned to Mackenzie, the young coach who came with Claiborne, and said, "Jim, would you like the job?"

"Yes sir, I sure would," he said. Broyles was still lucky.

Merrill Green came with us from Missouri to coach the offensive backs. We retained Dixie White from Jack Mitchell's staff as the offensive line coach, and Steed White as the B-team coach. We had to have a defensive backfield coach, and I remembered everybody telling me what a great coach Doug Dickey would make. He'd been a freshman at Florida when I was there with Bob Woodruff. Doug was in the Army at Colorado Springs, and he couldn't get out. He'd completed one tour of duty, but had signed up for another three-year hitch. I talked to his commanding general, and the general quite frankly told me he wouldn't let Doug out of the Army. "That

"The first thing I did after accepting the Arkansas job was to go looking for a great defensive coach, and I came up with Jim Mackenzie."

boy is going to be a general some day," the general said. Well, after hearing that I had to get him. I talked to Senator Bill Fulbright about it, and he spoke to the Secretary of the Army. We were told that the only way Doug could get out of the Army was to take a teaching job. We asked the school to request his release in order for him to become an instructor. He was assigned to teach in the PE Department, and we paid his salary to be a football coach.

On Barnie's recommendation, I hired Wilson Matthews, who'd built one of the most amazing high school coaching records in America at Central High of Little Rock. Without a doubt, Wilson's toughness, his approach to discipline, was just what I needed at that stage. I hated to discipline players unless they just carried me to the brink; then I'd usually overreact. Wilson encouraged everybody, players and coaches alike, to be mentally tough. Wilson had a practice field voice that could flay the hide off a mule. He'd usually center his attention on one player per practice and ride that youngster without letup. He always "got right" with the player before the day was done, with a wink or a joke or something to take off the sting.

Wilson taught our players to sing to the tune of "The Old Gray Mare," a song that proclaimed: "We don't give a damn for the whole

"I often called on my Georgia Tech form for pick-up baskbetball games with the staff at old Barnhill Fieldhouse."

state of Texas, we're from Arkansas." His raging enthusiasm was contagious. Say, for example, we were playing Baylor. Wilson would point to the Bear mascot patrolling the sidelines. "You see that big bear over there?" he'd scream at our players. "Well, I just want to run over there and kick him in the (censored). Now, tell me, ARE WE GONNA RIDE A WILD HORSE TONIGHT?"

At Central High, Wilson had a "fourth quarter class" of spring conditioning, and he talked us into starting one at Arkansas. It's a common thing now, but I think we may have been the first college team to set up an off-season program along these exact lines.

No new football staff ever walked into a sounder "support" situation than we found in old Barnhill Fieldhouse. Barnie's staff in those days included George Cole, Ab Bidwell, ticket manager Goldie Jones, sports information director Bob Cheyne, and trainer Bill "Ground Hog" or "Groundy" Ferrell.

Over the years it became fashionable to call George Cole "a great detail man" or "the best detail man in the business." People meant well, and George was indeed a great detail man, but it seems so shallow and patronizing to stop there. George was unique. He was loved and trusted all over the state; he knew everybody. He'd been a Razorback football hero in the 1920s, and he'd been an assistant to five head coaches: Fred Thomsen, Barnie, Otis Douglas, Bowden Wyatt, and Jack Mitchell. Out of his sense of duty and loyalty, George served a year as interim head coach during a hopeless wartime situation in 1942. In 1958, he'd just left the field to devote all his time to fund-raising and administration—duties that eventually went to Wilson Matthews and Lon Ferrell after George replaced Barnie as athletic director in 1967. It's hard to define George's role. He did what needed to be done, large or small. One day he might map out some far-reaching policy alternatives for Barnie's consideration, and the next he might drive to Brinkley or Lake Village, or Little Rock or Texarkana to reassure some anxious parent or put some wounded booster in a good humor.

Bill Ferrell arrived at Arkansas with Otis Douglas' regime in 1950, and stayed until he died of leukemia in 1967. On paper, Groundy was the athletic trainer and baseball coach, but that doesn't begin to scratch the surface. "He had no business being a trainer at Arkansas," Jim Lindsey said recently when Groundy's name popped up in a conversation. "He could have been a United States Senator or the president of a large corporation with ease. He could have been anything he wanted to be. And yet he took his job as seriously as if he were a preacher out on the mission field." There's no way we could calculate the games Groundy won for us by counteracting psychological hang-ups that went through youngsters' minds. He was brilliant.

"If a player was half-hurt, he was also half-well," Lindsey said. "He could play, but he didn't know he could play. Groundy would tell him something that would make him so mad at Groundy he'd be determined to go out and show him. And in showing him, he proved to himself he could play. Or Groundy would tell him what some other kid did—who in the past had gone out and played great with a pinched nerve in his neck or something. One of his favorite terms was *tender*. Like, he'd say to me, 'I had great hopes for you, Lindsey, but damned if I don't believe you're too tender.' I had a

"Bill Ferrell was more than a trainer; he was a father confessor and a master psychologist."

broken rib." If Bill Ferrell saw a youngster heading the wrong way, either as a football player or as a person, he always made it a point to get him off to one side and talk to him. No Razorback ever wanted Groundy to be disappointed with him.

When I arrived at Arkansas, my first mistake was jumpinig on football's latest vogue, the winged-T. Dave Nelson devised it at Delaware and Forest Evashevski popularized it with success at Iowa. I could see us running our belly series with the winged-T. I hired Dave Nelson to come down in the spring and help us put it in. The winged-T was a finesse offense, full of slow-developing sweeps and counters. We had been accustomed to the quick, simple belly option, and anyway you're always going to win first with your defense and kicking. I oversold myself on somebody else's offense, and I oversold myself on our players, two natural mistakes inexperienced coaches have been making for 100 years or so.

Oh, but what a honeymoon, football-wise, we had that first spring and summer before reality set in. We recruited one of the greatest freshman teams in the school's history. I toured the state meeting the fans and overselling the winged-T. During my rounds of Razorback Club fish-frys that year, I discovered Arkansas catfish. Back in Georgia, muddy-water catfish were throwaways. As soon as I tasted the Arkansas variety, I ate more catfish steaks at one sitting than you could believe. I'd be back there sampling all the time they were cooking. I literally ate so much I'd make myself sick.

Elmer "B" Lindsey, a hot halfback from Forrest City, Jim's older brother, became the first athlete to "pledge" Arkansas for us, but a few weeks later, B signed a bonus baseball contract with the St. Louis Cardinals. About the time we knew we were losing Lindsey, we realized we might have a chance at Lance Alworth, an authentic national blue-chipper from Brookhaven, Mississippi. Lance signed early with Ole Miss (as most Mississippi blue-chippers did), but when he married his high school sweetheart he came up against Mississippi's no-marriage policy for scholarship football players. With an athlete of Alworth's potential, the school was willing to try to work around its rule. Lance could go to school on a baseball scholarship and go out for football, but his pride was stung and he didn't want to do it that way.

I pulled out all the stops. I'd never involved Barbara in recruiting before—and would only one time in the future—but I took her to Mississippi with me for a week. She visited Betty Alworth and her parents while I played golf with Lance and his father. We went on to Memphis where Lance was a prominent player in the high school All-Star game they used to hold there each summer. One night we were going to dinner, and Mr. Alworth said, "How about some seafood, Frank? I know a great place."

"Terrific," I said.

"I love raw oysters, Frank. How about you?"

"Oh, sure. Absolutely." (I could never bring myself to try to eat one before, but you can bet I wolfed 'em down that evening.)

They came to Fayetteville for a visit, and we were on the golf course when I first allowed myself to think that Lance was coming with us. He asked if it could be worked out so they could stay an extra day. Trying to restrain myself from jumping 12 feet in the air and giving a war whoop, I said, "Why, yes, I think that can be arranged without any problem."

Well, I'm sure you know Lance played on our three straight championship teams, 1959-60-61, and made All-American, and followed up as one of the all-time pass-catching stars in pro football. He gave our image a great lift before he even played a game. He represented a real breakthrough for us; Arkansas wasn't accustomed to going into neighboring states and coming away with national blue-chippers.

By this time, the Razorbacks pretty well had an edge on the recruiting of almost any Arkansas prospect. The state had closed its ranks around the program. Out-of-state recruiting usually meant finding a few players in the Memphis area, or in parts of Missouri, Oklahoma, and Kansas, that were close to Fayetteville. It would be another year or two before we made any headway in Texas.

Because of a one-year adjustment in the schedule, we opened with Baylor instead of a non-conference opponent, and played Rice in the No. 4 slot, where we normally met Baylor. Arkansas fans had a lot of things to turn over in their minds that September—the winged-T, a league game for an opener, and all those fine freshmen—and they were excited. So was I.

In front of a War Memorial Stadium sellout crowd on the dreary, foggy evening of September 20, 1958, we made a total of 33 yards and three first downs. We did not make a first down the first half. A Baylor team headed for a last-place finish in the Southwest Conference beat us 12-0. In the second half, we did some kicking on third down, figuring our best bet was to punt Baylor back and hope for a fumble. When we did that, some fan jumped up and hollered, "Hell, we might as well have Barnhill back!"

The next day, I went to Little Rock to do my television show. The Fayetteville airport was weathered in, so I asked Dixie White to drive with me. We talked out our offensive problems eight hours without letup, coming and going. We agreed we were going to have to drop all the winged-T and stick with the belly series. The winged-T required big, strong linemen who could maintain blocks; our linemen were small and quick. The winged-T required seasoned linemen who could absorb all the pulling and trapping assignments. We didn't have that much experience on our squad.

We didn't announce it to the world, of course, but we greatly modified and simplified our system. The big-yardage play in the winged-T was supposed to be the counter criss-cross. We tried it once against Baylor, and our halfbacks, Jim Mooty and Don Horton, collided in the backfield. The next week Tulsa beat us, but we looked a little better. We played above ourselves against TCU but lost, 12-7. About that time, Jim Mooty, our best runner, left the squad and went home to El Dorado. His pride was hurt when he was dropped off the first team in what was an ill-calculated move to try to make him go harder in practice. I mishandled that episode from start to finish— another mark of inexperience. Anyway, Jim came right back and worked his way from the sixth team to the top in a matter of days.

According to all our coaches, the 1958 Rice game was the worst we ever played. About midway through the second quarter, Jim Mackenzie turned to me and said, "Frank, neither team is good enough to win this game." Rice won, though, 24-0. We were awful; we couldn't do anything. We played at Fayetteville, and after the game Governor Orval Faubus walked into our dressing room. ".Coach Broyles," he said, "I want to tell you what a good job your're doing. I like the way your players play."

"Just what I've always wanted," I thought. "A governor who doesn't know anything about football."

After that, we became fast friends.

Mooty was back in the line-up when we went to Austin to play Texas. We lost, 24-6, but we looked better. Jim gave us some zip. He was coming on as the "fly man" in our system—a wingback who started in motion at high speed back toward the play, and usually wound up with the ball. In our other set, we'd run Jim off tackle with the belly power play. He was a 165-pounder with all the heart, fire, and cutting ability in the world. Darrell Royal, then in his second year at the University of Texas, gave me a little pep talk on the field before the game. "You're doing a good job," he said. "Your team's getting better. Everybody knows you can coach. This is rebuilding. This is just your first year. You're on the right track." I'd known Darrell casually since his days at Mississippi State when he'd visit us at Georgia Tech in the spring. He wanted to look into all aspects of Tech's kicking game, he said; when he played for Bud Wilkinson at Oklahoma, the Sooners scored so many points they almost never had to kick.

One day at Tech, we'd had a two-hour chat about incorporating the belly series into Darrell's OU split-T, and I'd been totally impressed with his soundness. Ironically, one of the last straws in my decision to leave Tech came when some Longhorn people called Bobby Dodd to see if he had any interest in the vacant Texas job after the '56 season. Dodd couldn't see leaving Atlanta at that stage of his career, and the job ultimately went to Darrell, my contemporary. Darrell had already been a head coach three years, at Mississippi State and Washington, and this was one of the factors that made me feel I was falling far behind.

I appreciated Darrell's words at Austin, but I wasn't at all sure he was correct. By this time, I was down from 195 pounds to 170. Just before the Texas game, I had a notice from the income tax people to come in for an interview. Something minor, just a clarification of some item, but I told Barbara, "I might as well go to jail. In fact, I hope they put me in jail." I wrote my daddy and told him to save me a place in the insurance business. "I'll be home much earlier than you think, and I'll need a job," I told him.

We went into the Ole Miss game 0-5 and the Rebels were, as usual, 5-0. We fell behind, 14-0, and missed a 14-14 tie when Jim Monroe's two-point conversion pass went just beyond Mooty's grasp. For the first time, we had an attack. Mooty ripped around over the field like a wildcat. He gained 120 yards, and Monroe was settling down and taking charge at quarterback. Fighting Ole Miss to the wire, 14-12, encouraged us and encouraged our fans, but a moral victory is not the real thing. We stood 0-6. My personal losing streak was nine, going back to the Oklahoma-Missouri game the previous year.

Dixie White had been at Arkansas three years with Jack Mitchell. On the field at College Station before the Texas A&M game, I asked Dixie if he thought Arkansas could ever compete consistently in the Southwest Conference. "At one time I thought so," Dixie said. "I thought we could be average or better most of the time, and sneak through and win it every once in a while. Now, I don't know. I don't see any way we can compete with all these Texas athletes they pick from."

Arkansas recovered a fumble at the Aggie 16. From the eight, Monroe went the wrong way. He rolled left and the other backs went right. A busted play let Jim walk into the end zone. I turned to Dixie. "I don't see how we can lose this one," I said.

Texas A&M led at the half, 8-7. We goofed again on the second-half kickoff. Joe Paul Alberty went to the left; his wall of blockers formed on the right. Alberty reached the Aggies' 20. "You see, Dixie?" I said. "We can't lose this one." The Razorbacks won it, 21-8. When people start asking about our greatest victories at Arkansas, they are surprised when I mention this one. It's a matter of record. We waited longer for it than any other.

We won our last four games in '58, and rode the carryover to three straight championships and four straight bowl trips.

Hardin-Simmons was a welcomed breather at Little Rock. Fans recall that game only for the fact that both Jim Mooty and Billy Kyser returned kickoffs 100 yards for touchdowns while we were wrapping it up, 60-15.

Barbara and I were building our house on Hope Street in Fayetteville. I heard that Darrell had built a house at Austin, so I said: "If he's got enough confidence to build a house, I have too." So we went ahead with it, and we were trying to get our house ready along with everything else. Barbara was pregnant, and having more trouble than usual, and I was coaching football (and having more trouble than usual), and the whole hectic pace of that year seems incredible when I look back on it.

While I was gone to the A&M game, Barbara moved us into our then half-completed new house. Her doctor told her the baby was going to be born early, and she'd better get into her new house. She was so big, I kept telling her there were two babies in there, or four, but the doctor said no, just one large one. She told the contractor she was moving in on November 1, which happened to be the date of our A&M game. She placed a stool at the entrance and told the movers, "This goes here, that goes there."

When I came in from the Hardin-Simmons game the next Saturday night, she said, "Well, we're in the house. Let the baby come." I didn't know what she was talking about. It was supposed to be another month. About eight o'clock Sunday morning, she said, "Frank, I'm ready to go to the hospital." I asked if she was having labor pains. "Yes, for three hours," she said. "I'm ready to go."

By then, after four boys, we were old pros. No panic; total calmness. I left her at the hospital, ran a few errands, and took the boys to Sunday School. When I got back to the hospital, she was already in the delivery room. I was sitting there about half asleep when they

"I passed out only a few seconds, but that's the true story of my first meeting with Linda and Betsy."

brought Barbara out on a stretcher down a little dimly lit corridor. "Well, doctor," I said, "did you come through for me and give me a little girl?" Dr. Jim Mashburn laughed and said yes. I looked under Barbara's right arm, and there was a pretty little girl. "Jim, thanks so much," I said to the doctor. "We really wanted a girl this time." Barbara said, "Frank, look over here." She had another pretty little girl on her left arm. I literally fainted. I would have hit the floor if the doctor hadn't caught me. I passed out only a few seconds, but that's the true story of my first meeting with Linda and Betsy.

The A&M and Hardin-Simmons victories were vital but, from the public's view, our first "big win" was a 13-6 upset of an SMU team that had a junior passing star named Don Meredith, and a good chance to go to the Cotton Bowl. We used four ends to rush Meredith and we just hoped we didn't get hurt in other areas. Kyser finally broke a 37-yard touchdown run down the sideline, and we sewed it up. Billy Kyser was one of those guys who could come in off the bench and give you a game-breaker.

Well, our November recovery in 1958 led to quite a dizzy little era. We tied for the championship in '59 with an 8-2 record and beat Georgia Tech in the Gator Bowl in one of those "master vs. pupil" match-ups, Dodd vs. Broyles, that have so much appeal. We won the SWC title outright in '60 with another 8-2 record, and lost to Duke in the Cotton Bowl, 7-6. We tied for first place again in '61, 8-2, and were matched with Bear Bryant's first national championship Alabama team in the Sugar Bowl. We battled the Tide to the wire and lost, 10-3.

In 1962, we won nine games during a season for the first time, but missed the championship by a half-game. Our reward was another Sugar Bowl trip, against Ole Miss. Some fans in those days said Johnny Vaught's Rebs held a "hex" over us. Some even said I demanded that the Ole Miss series be dropped. The Razorbacks went 0-6 against Mississippi in my time, but no "hex" was involved. We were way down when we met them in '58, and we lost by 14-12. The best of all the great Ole Miss teams beat us at Memphis in '59, 28-0. The record says we lost by 10-7 in '60; you can get arguments in Arkansas that it was a 7-7 tie. They beat us in the season-opening heat at Jackson in '61, 16-0, the first game in the new stadium there. That was the end of the regular season series. When you played Mississippi in those days, you were always up against one of the two or three best teams in the country. Always. Later, we lost to them twice in the Sugar Bowl, 17-13 after the '62 season and 27-22 after '69.

Barnie never liked the Ole Miss series. He dropped it once after a recruiting fuss with Ole Miss in the 1940s, and then renewed it because it was such a money maker, one of the few money makers Arkansas had in the lean years of the '40s and '50s. It was an old, intense, neighborhood rivalry and it generated much heat. Barnie believed that it distracted from what always had to be our No. 1 goal: compete and win in the Southwest Conference. The Rebels occupied the middle slot in our schedule between Texas and Texas A&M. Ole Miss officials suggested we move it to the top of the schedule (as we did in '61), but a season-opening opponent of Ole Miss's caliber was alien to Barnie's scheduling philosophy. He let the series lapse after '61. This was Barnie's decision, and it was rooted in events that took place long before I came to Arkansas. "Ole Miss is the kind of team you want to see in a bowl game," he said. "You don't want to turn around from Texas and look at 'em." (Incidentally, Ole Miss returns to the Arkansas schedule in the 1980s.)

Our early teams at Arkansas won on quickness and heart. With a few outstanding exceptions, we weren't blessed with a lot of great athletes. We didn't have the size and strength to overpower people on defense, so we developed the monster-slant defense, soon widely copied, which emphasized stunts and false looks and anything we could do to confuse a blocking scheme. We didn't have the size and strength to overpower people on offense, so we developed scramble blocking techniques that emphasized staying low and "getting in the other man's wheels."

These first few years represented a dream come ture to me as a young coach. To the fans of Arkansas, they meant much more. I can't explain it, but Arkansas people are different. They care more. Some claim all football fans are just alike the world over. They are not. Arkansas fans are different. Sometimes, when you're caught up in a big game at Little Rock or Fayetteville, you can actually feel that tie between the public and the team. I've never experienced that anywhere else.

I suppose a lot of it traces back to Arkansas' "step-child" status in an otherwise all-Texas conference, and to the lean years that made the Razorbacks perpetual underdoogs. We were underdogs more often than not while we won three straight championships, and I think it would be safe to say the Razorbacks are the greatest force for unity and common purpose that our state ever had.

While we were getting ready for the 1959 Gator Bowl, speculative stories started popping up that I was on my way to the University of Florida. Bob Woodruff had left the field to confine himself to being athletic director at Florida, and I suppose the rumors stemmed from my association with Bob at Baylor and Florida. I

"Our early teams at Arkansas won on quickness and heart."

denied it so emphatically that I never had much problem with job-switching rumors afterwards (the Florida job eventually went to Ray Graves). I wrote out a statement shortly after that, and kept it with me for two or three years. Bob Cheyne also had a copy in case Dodd retired at Georgia Tech and I couldn't be immediately reached by the media. The statement said flatly I would have no interest in the Tech job, although I tried to word it in a way that would avoid hurting anyone's feelings. When Dodd knew he was going to retire, he called and asked if I would be interested in the job. This happened early in 1967.

"No, Coach," I said. "I'm completely happy at Arkansas. I'm not leaving."

"That's what I thought," he said. "You've got a great situation there, Frank."

Later on, some friends and former teammates of mine in Georgia approached me with an offer anyway. Under the terms submitted for my consideration in January of 1972 was a fantastic package underwritten by Tech alumni, not the school. It would have exceeded $2 million over a six-year period. However, Barbara expressed our feelings at the time when she said, "We can't be bought."

Georgia Tech was the only school that ever actually offered me a job while I coached at Arkansas. I'd get feelers from time to time from this or that school, but everybody soon got the idea and started going after our assistant coaches instead. In time, 11 of my assistants moved directly into head-coaching positions: Hayden Fry (SMU), Doug Dickey (Tennessee), Jim Mackenzie (Oklahoma), Bill Pace (Vanderbilt), Johnny Majors (Iowa State), Hootie Ingram (Clemson), Charley Coffey (Virginia Tech), Billy Kinard (Ole Miss), Richard Williamson (Memphis State), Bo Rein (North Carolina State), and Bill Lewis (Wyoming). Once this trend established itself, it became quite a recruiting tool for us. I refer to the recruiting of coaches. Time after time we'd lose an outstanding coach and attract his replacement from a flourishing program elsewhere. A coaching staff needs the stability of veterans steeped in the ways of the program, but it also needs the zeal and fresh ideas of young coaches on the way up. We were usually able to maintain the proper balance.

Gosh, we had some great staffs. Beginning with the first one. Jim Mackenzie was a smiling genius, a seemingly tireless worker, and his football mind was brilliant. Doug Dickey was that officer-type leader: intelligent, articulate, observant. Relatively new to coaching, Jim and Doug came with few preconceptions. The staff's seasoning was provided by Dixie White, a veteran line coach, and Wilson Matthews, with his overall experience and expertise in toughness and discipline.

Merrill Green, my first offensive backfield coach, left for Texas Tech after 1960, and we brought in Hayden Fry from Baylor. I'd coached Hayden when I worked for Bob Woodruff. Hayden contributed a lot to our staff in the one season he served before he landed the head-coaching job at SMU. When Hayden left, I moved Dickey from the secondary to offense, and brought in Bill Pace from Kansas for the secondary. When Doug went to Tennessee, we moved Pace to offense and brought in Johnny Majors from Tennessee for the secondary. When Bill Pace took the Vanderbilt job, Majors went to offense and then became a head coach at Iowa State (and Pitt and Tennessee). Four of the brightest young coaches in America gained the invaluable background of both defensive and offensive responsibility, and of course, Arkansas reaped the dividends.

Mervin Johnson, who'd been my team captain at Missouri, came with us as a coaching beginner at Arkansas in '58, and returned to Missouri for two years. He came back in '62, replacing Dixie White. Mervin was my right arm for many, many years. He had an easy, patient personality, and he would mesh with me and calm me down. With him around, I just calmed down automatically. He was closer to me personally than any other coach I've ever had. Over the years, Mervin handled a variety of responsibilities on our staff, and did a first-rate job with all of them. Any time we seemed to be having problems in a certain area, people assumed Mervin would soon turn up there. They were usually right.

An incident that led to Dixie White's leaving taught me a great lesson about holding my cool. In November of 1961, we took our team to Eureka Springs the night before our game at Fayetteville with Texas A&M. That was the closest place we could get hotel rooms for the team as we had already started our practice of going somewhere to isolate it from fans, friends, students, and all types of distractions in the 24 hours before kickoff. On this trip we boarded a bus and went up through Huntsville on the winding road to Eureka. We had to stop and unload to cross a bridge that wouldn't bear the weight of both the bus and the passengers. Everybody cheered when the empty bus crossed without mishap, and we climbed back on.

That night, during a routine check of the rooms, Hayden Fry found Lance Alworth, Darrell Williams, and one or two others playing poker in the wee hours. The next morning, the coaches were discussing what disciplinary measures we were going to take. Nerves were frayed to begin with because we had to beat A&M in order to have any chance at a third straight championship. Dixie told me it was my fault, that I was too easy on the players all the time. I lost my temper and came down hard on him. I told him I'd never noticed him running over to the dormitory and checking on the discipline and so forth. I totally overreacted.

At the game, Dixie never opened his mouth. Somebody else had to take over the offensive line. We won 15-8, and Dixie coached on to the end of the season, then took an assistant's job at LSU. I'll never forget how sick I was that day; I didn't know what to do. Regardless of what he said, I should not have reacted as I did. I should have waited until I cooled off, and we could have discussed it in a calm, rational way. My temper put the team's best interest in jeopardy.

Another regret from the early years concerns Bruce Fullerton, one of the great running backs in Arkansas high school history. Bruce came in with our first freshmen group, and he was a key to our recruiting that first year. We had to get him; he was a can't miss prospect on a level with Alworth. Bruce was primarily a ball-carrier. In those days we were trying to set up our program, trying to teach the kids they had to be tough, complete players: block, tackle, play offense, play defense. We couldn't afford to have anybody who wasn't able do it all. That was the mistake I made; I should have recognized that Bruce wasn't cut out to be a defensive player and used him just for what he could do best. And that was to score with the football.

If I'd had more experience as a head coach, I wouldn't have been as influenced by "Well, he's not tackling!" or "Well, he's not blocking!" I should have said, "That's all right. He scores with the football and we'll give him the ball and use him accordingly." We kept trying to make Bruce a two-way player, and he grew so frustrated he finally gave up football after his sophomore year. This was one of my worst mistakes in dealing with people, and I wish I'd had enough experience at the time to overcome it.

On the subject of disciplinary flaps, I recall that one season one of our assistants discovered two or three of the players were secretly maintaining an off-campus apartment. When I confronted them, they said it was just a place to go and rest under the air-conditioning between two-a-day workouts. They wouldn't dream of using it to break training in any way. "Coach, you can drop in to see us any time of the night or day," one of them said. "And you can bring Mrs. Broyles with you. We'd be happy to see both of you." I declined with thanks, and told them I didn't want to hear anything else about an apartment. The picture they drew didn't jibe with reports I'd picked up elsewhere.

We were all so proud when Doug Dickey landed the head-coaching job at Tennessee. Especially Barnie. Barnie's alma mater took a head coach from Arkansas, Bowden Wyatt, who was like a son to him, and it pleased Barnie no end that Tennessee later came back to our program for an assistant coach. This was, I guess, an indication that Arkansas had reached a new level of prestige. Tennessee and Oklahoma were football powers long before Arkansas. Two years after Doug left, Oklahoma also drew a head coach off the Razorbacks' staff.

It didn't surprise me that Doug had success at Tennessee immediately. I felt pretty sure he would get the job if Bob Woodruff became athletic director at Tennessee because Doug had been Bob's fair-haired boy at Florida. Doug played as a non-passing college quarterback, and then, after four years of firing passes at our defensive backs, he reached a point where he could throw the ball like a bullet. "If you're interested," I told him, "I think I can get you a $100,000 job as a pro quarterback." When some Tennessee people made their first approach to Doug, I advised him to tell them he wouldn't be interested until the school had an official vacancy. That really impressed them.

In May of 1967, after an opening season at Oklahoma that included victories over both Texas and Nebraska, Jim Mackenzie died of a heart attack at the age of 38. The last gathering of my original 1958 staff took place at Jim's funeral in Norman. Although he worked in a profession where 12-hour days for months at a time are standard, Jim always drove himself far beyond ordinary limits. On game days he'd smoke five packs of cigarettes. Jim could always work out a defense to stop anybody. This carried beyond football. Jim was determined to beat me in golf and he finally figured out a way. He "slow played" me to a three-and-two victory for a club championship at Fayetteville. I rode the cart, but he walked. I grew so frustrated waiting for him that I couldn't do anything. We were out there for hours.

When Jim left for Oklahoma after the 1965 season, we hired Charley Coffey from Tennessee as our defensive coordinator. I guess Coffey was the best fundamental coach I ever had. He was also the hardest worker and the most intense. He'd work until midnight every night, and he couldn't sleep past five o'clock in the morning. Workaholic is not a strong enough term. He was actually a slave to his profession. He worried and fretted and smoked at least as many cigarettes as Jim.

Coffey hated our monster scheme of defense. He coached it at Tennessee under Doug, but he hated it. He wanted to coach the 4-3, a derivation of the 6-2. He persuaded me finally, and we went to that defense in '68 with tremendous success. He felt more comfortable with it, and did a magnificent job. Coffey and I had quite a "discussion" about defensing the wishbone, which I'll explain when we get into the Texas series.

We won the first 21 games when Johnny Majors was on our staff. Johnny didn't really taste adversity until '67 when he coached the offense through a 4-5-1 year with an unsettled quarterback situation. Other than Wilson Matthews, Richard Williamson was the toughest coach on the field I ever had—the most demanding of his players, the best disciplinarian. Fred Akers and Barry Switzer, who now oppose one another in the Texas-Oklahoma rivalry, were Arkansas teammates and seniors on the '59 team. They started their coaching careers as graduate aides, helping with our freshmen in '60. Barry stayed and became a full-time coach with us before he went with Jim Mackenzie to Oklahoma in '66. Fred coached high school football in Texas before joining Darrell's staff as an assistant. After being successful on his own at Wyoming and winning a Fiesta Bowl trip (against one of Barry's Oklahoma teams), Fred was selected by Texas to be Darrell's successor.

Jimmy Johnson, another of our Arkansas players, later came back to coach with us (from Barry's OU staff) and is now the head coach at Oklahoma State.

Which was our strongest staff? The group we started with in '58 would be hard to beat. Our staff during the '64-'65 winning streak, however, would also be hard to beat (Mackenzie, Mervin Johnson, Majors, Matthews, Pace, Switzer, Steed White, Jack Davis, and Lon Ferrell). Our staff in the 1968-69 revival was equally superb (Coffey, Don Breaux, Hootie Ingram, Williamson, Mervin Johnson, Harold Horton, Davis, and Ferrell). And yet how could anyone forget the quality of our '75 staff (Bo Rein, Jimmy Johnson, Bill Lewis, Frank Falks, Don Boyce, Jesse Branch, Horton, Ken Turner, Steve Sprayberry, and Joe Fred Young).

I never minded searching for good coaches to replace good coaches. I looked forward to it, actually. Moreover, after my own frustrations as an assistant, I felt elated each time one of our men got a job. The most meaningful compliment to our program was the fact that our assistant coaches were always in demand when quality jobs came open. Obviously we were doing something right at Arkansas.

11
THE SEARCH FOR WINNERS

Recruiting is and will remain an inexact and highly speculative science, to say the least, but there was a time when coaches had a more reasonable margin for error. From the beginning, we knew Arkansas athletes would always be the backbone of the Razorback program. We also knew we had to recruit selectively outside the state if we were to develop into a consistent national power rather than a once-in-a-while longshot in the Southwest Conference.

When our program flourished in the early and middle 1960s, we were taking 30 to 35 Arkansas freshmen a year, plus several good Texas players, plus a scattering of prospects in other neighboring states. The Arkansas athletes were hungry, motivated, and involved —eager to be part of a new frontier for their state and their school. With no limit on scholarships, we'd take 30 or 35 and hope 15 or 20 matured to a point where they could help us when they were juniors and seniors. Many of them were redshirted—given an extra year to develop as football players and students. Until Bill Montgomery started as a sophomore in 1968, all our winning quarterbacks had the benefit of an extra year: James Monroe, George McKinney, Billy Moore, Fred Marshall and Jon Brittenum.

Players just didn't start as "natural" sophomores in those days, unless they had the exceptional gifts of a Wayne Harris, a Lance Alworth, a Loyd Phillips, or Harry Jones. Freshmen, of course, weren't even eligible for the varsity. A lot of people, especially Eastern sports columnists, used to slash away at redshirting, and I never understood what all the fuss was about. The system benefited the student-athlete more than anything else.

When we first came to Arkansas, we drew very little attention from either the high school coach or the athlete in Texas. In fact, we got zilch, zero, none. The good Texas athletes wouldn't even talk to us. They had no interest in Arkansas. They had no interest in setting a precedent, and we were very disappointed. After we won the Gator Bowl in 1959, after we beat Texas at Austin, 24-23, in a great game on regional television in '60, and went on to the Cotton Bowl, the situation improved.

Jerry Lamb was the first outstanding Texas athlete we recruited. I remember Doug Dickey telling the story that he was in the study hall waiting for Jerry, when he saw a Texas coach coming. Doug said, "Jerry, let's go ride around and get a Coke" (which was legal then), and he maneuvered Lamb off the campus before the Texas coach saw him. Signing took place the next day, and Lamb signed with us. His signing was a breakthrough. Because we got Lamb, we were also able to sign Ronnie Caveness from the same Houston school. When Lamb and Caveness became great players for us and we won some championships, we gained the attention of Texas boys. In addition, we had our high school clinic which eventually drew 150 to 200 Texas high school coaches a year. Everything meshed.

Texas sportswriters were very fair to our Arkansas program. It seemed they'd rather have Texas boys go to Arkansas and stay in the Southwest Conference instead of leaving for Oklahoma or somewhere else, and we capitalized on that feeling. We recruited some great players in Texas, and we finished second on a lot of other great ones. Distance hurt us. When we came up head-to-head with the University of Texas on a player, we lost most of the time. So did everybody else, but UT couldn't take them all. The state of Texas contains about 1100 high school teams, so in theory you start with 1100 players at each position. Texas high school football is a legend that doesn't need to be dwelled on here, but it supplies a dozen or more major schools in Texas and adds substantially to the squads of a dozen others outside the state.

Occupying the driver's seat, Texas always pushed for early commitments from its top choices. Darrell would flatly tell kids: "We've got a scholarship for you. If you don't want it, somebody else down the street does." Darrell wasn't interested in taking a recruiting battle down to the last ditch, and I don't blame him. He might lose more that way than by pressing for a decision a month before the signing

"Seniors Lance Alworth (left) and Dean Garrett (right) help recruit a great punter, Bobby Nix."

date. Some turned him down and we'd get in on those, but usually Texas attracted the boys Darrell really wanted. That was a fact of life.

My pitch to out-of-state athletes (and Arkansas youngsters as well) was that we didn't have many distractions. Distractions, in this case, meant "good times." We had enough good times to go with the environment in Fayetteville. We sold the small classroom, the interested teacher, the concerned counselor who would know he was an athlete and help him adjust his schedule or arrange tutoring so he could stay up with other students. Parents liked this smalltown atmosphere, and that was our basic appeal to Texas boys. We often found athletes who were looking to get away from the bigness of Houston or Dallas or the other cities, and we usually stood a good chance because we were just the opposite.

In Arkansas, we signed the obvious prospects and then spent the spring and summer checking back on "sleepers," late developers. We granted a lot of one-year scholarships. Searching for boys who might have grown some or added some quickness after football season, we ran across Randy Stewart at Magnet Cove in the early '60s. Randy was a red-headed, freckle-faced youngster who had enough size to be a prospect. We talked to him about a one-year football scholarship, and he accepted it. Later we learned he had a merit scholarship to any school he wanted to attend. We knew he was a fine student, but we didn't realize he'd already been nominated as a merit scholar. He came to us slow-footed and quick-tempered. He worked on weights, however, and did everything he could in and out of season to improve himself. The result was that he developed into an all-conference football player—the starting center on our undefeated teams of 1964 and '65—and his grade point average led the engineering school.

Randy then joined Exxon and has been moved and promoted with the rapidity you see when large corporations prepare someone for a high executive position. I'm told that he heads his company's entire operation in Alaska. I've always marveled at a youngster who would take a one-year football scholarship and give up a four-year academic scholarship, which he had earned.

At Smackover we found Bobby Burnett, the first of the three Burnett brothers. We gave him a one-year scholarship because he impressed us with the way he ran the hurdles in the state high school meet in May. You never saw such quickness. Each year, he'd make a run at a position, and something would happen. Either he'd get hurt, or he'd fumble the ball, and he'd be put back. He had the quickness and determination, but we'd see things in him that we couldn't depend on. Each year, he received a one-year extension on his scholarship. Jim Mackenzie had recruited him and, coming up to Bobby's fourth year in school, Jim wanted to push him up or push him out. "Frank, why are you giving him another chance?" Jim asked one day. "Can he play?"

"We've just got to," I said. "He's got the quickness and the ability and I never saw anybody who wanted to play more. Someday he's gonna find himself. You don't know how many times he's been in my office with tears in his eyes, afraid we'd give up on him. He cares too much. Something good is gonna happen for him."

Bobby broke in as the alternate tailback behind Jackie Brasuell, on our national championship team in 1964. The last half of that season, Bobby became a great football player and, as a senior in '65 (when we went 10-0 again), he carried the ball 200 times without losing a fumble, and then was the American Football League rookie of the year for Buffalo. A tremendous young man, a tremendous athlete, and yet he was stymied until his fourth and fifth years in school.

We gave his brother Tommy a one-year scholarship, and he became a fine receiver for us. Then little Bill Burnett came along, a youngster who looked less a football player than anyone I've ever seen. By this time, the family had moved to Bentonville (their father, Clell Burnett, was a teacher, school adminstrator, and former coach), and I'd seen Bill play against Fayetteville High School. I didn't want to, but I offered him a one-year scholarship.

Toward the end of Bill's last year in high school, Bobby and Tommy came to my office to talk to me one day. "Coach, I didn't deserve any more than a one-year opportunity," Bobby said. "That was fine for me."

"I hadn't done anything in high school," Tommy said. "I didn't deserve more than a one-year opportunity."

Then they said Bill deserved a four-year scholarship. Somewhere during the conversation, it came out that Tulsa had offered him a four-year scholarship, and that Bill would probably take it. A Burnett brother wearing an enemy uniform into Razorback Stadium? Unthinkable. "Well, I think you're right," I told Bobby and Tommy. "We'll give Bill a four-year scholarship." So he broke all our scoring records, and if he hadn't been hurt late in his senior season, 1970, there's no telling how that year might have turned out.

Bobby Crockett came to school on a one-year scholarship. So did Glen Ray Hines and Mike Bender. I could go on and on. It might be fun sometime to sit down and pick an all-time Razorback line-up of players who first enrolled in school with no more than a one-year guarantee. It could be virtually an All-American squad.

We had to change much of our recruiting philosophy in the late '60s. In the name of raising academic standards, the NCAA required prospective scholarship athletes to "predict," according to their class rank. A youngster who had only a C average in high school would have to score high on his College Boards to qualify for a scholarship. A C average isn't bad for an athlete, when you consider how much of his time is consumed by practicing, playing, and traveling. If he came from a good school, or if he came from a small class that had a lot of As and Bs, he ranked low in his class and would have to make a higher College Board score.

The practical effect was to cut us from 30-35 Arkansas boys a year to about 10 or 12. We couldn't get the blue-chippers out of Texas we'd been finding in the past. We were knocked down in both quality and quantity. We were shutting out 15 to 20 percent of the top athletes we had a chance to get. An athlete who could "predict" had to be our prime consideration."

Anyone who has spent any time close to athletics can supply an endless list of players who came out of high school as poor academic risks, and maybe poor citizenship risks, and eventually became lawyers, teachers, business executives, you name it—solid community leaders, exemplary people. Some of them would not have "predicted."

Texas still got the top athlete, the top student-athlete, because there were so many athletes in Texas, but we couldn't. One year we could find only eight Arkansas prospects we wanted who could also qualify academically. Arkansas high schools in the smaller communities were generally at a disadvantage financially compared to schools in Texas and the larger Arkansas districts. The better financed districts, quite logically, generally produced students more prepared for the College Board scores.

Our squads dropped off before the limit of 30 freshmen came along in 1974. The 30-limit has not hurt us as much as I anticipated, and it may have helped in some instances. Oklahoma can only take 30, for example, so we might go into Oklahoma for a player or two the Sooners would otherwise have signed. The schools in Texas can take only 30 each, and no matter how selective they are, they can't take all the blue-chippers in Texas. It's a plain fact our program picked up again after the 30-limit came in. Our '75 squad went to the Cotton Bowl, and Lou Holtz's first two teams, in '77 and '78, went 11-1 and 9-2-1 and earned trips to the Orange and Fiesta bowls.

Freshmen became eligible for varsity competition in 1972 and "made" our team immediately that year, and have made it every season since. Just a few years earlier, as I've noted, it was considered rare for sophomores to play.

We did not recruit black athletes until the late '60s. When I came to Arkansas there were no black players in the Southwest Conference or in the Southeastern. Nothing written in a Board policy stated that we were to avoid recruiting blacks, but it was very clearly (though informally) conveyed to me by the Board that we would not. I recruited the first black football players at the University of Missouri. I never mentioned that fact as a rebuttal to a few who charged that I was dragging my feet on integration, and certainly I never cited the implicit policy of the Board. I knew athletic integration was inevitable, and I felt it was just and right, but it was a matter out of my hands and I didn't think about it a great deal. I assume there was a feeling on the part of some of our Board members that if we unilaterally integrated our athletic program, Southeastern Conference schools would use it against us and open up recruiting strongholds in certain areas of Arkansas.

We fell behind. The Southwest and Southeastern conferences fell behind. Then SMU recruited Jerry Levias in 1965. That was the breakthrough in the Southwest. All at once it became an issue, and people wanted to know why we weren't recruiting black athletes. By then, it was hard to explain. It was also hard to recruit black athletes. Our conference had an image to overcome. In the last two or three years, I think we've caught up with our recruiting competition from the Big Eight and Big Ten and other leagues that had successfully recruited Southern blacks for years. I think the Southeastern Conference may still be behind; they were even later than our league in integrating.

Jon Richardson, a running back from Little Rock Horace Mann High School, became our first black scholarship football player in 1969.

We had some limited success in attracting black players the next few years. Our image in this area improved considerably in 1974 when we were able to recruit Ike Forte, a widely sought junior college black from Texarkana, Texas, and Jerry Eckwood of Brinkley, a high school star who literally could have gone to school anywhere in the United States. Ike and Jerry were (until Eckwood suffered an injury in midseason) the starting veer backs on our '75 championship team. About the same time, Eddie Sutton started building a national basketball power around Sidney Moncrief of Little Rock, Ron Brewer of Fort Smith, and Marvin Delph of Conway. These teams, and these players, erased our last identification problems with black youngsters and their families in Arkansas.

The old image possibly still hampers our football and basketball recruiting of black players in other parts of the country, much to our regret. No athletic program can ever be better than its recruiting, or, more to the point, the quality of its recruits. Any coach who doubts that soon finds himself in another line of work.

12
THREE STEPS FROM A DYNASTY

Question: "If you could pick one victory that meant more to the Razorbacks' football program than any other, which would it be?" In one form or another, I've been asked that many times, especially since my retirement from coaching. I can't answer it. I can't pick one. I can't pick 10. I might pick 30, but what would that prove?

Beating Texas A&M in 1958, when we were so low and beginning to wonder about everything, was as important to us as any other game we won. That got us started. Beating TCU in the rain at Fayetteville in 1959, 3-0 on Fred Akers' field goal, was definitely a milestone for us. The Horned Frogs were the defending champions, and that game convinced us we could win, and also gave others around the Southwest Conference an idea that we were for real. Dutch Meyer, the retired TCU coach who did a football column at that time, was sufficiently impressed to call us a contender.

The SMU game at Dallas later that year belongs close to the top. Several thousand Razorback fans caught the last special football train ever chartered out of Arkansas to see what we could do about Don Meredith. With Jim Mooty hurt, Lance Alworth, Jim Monroe, and Joe Paul Alberty staged the greatest running show I ever saw in one-platoon, unspecialized football. We ran for 400 yards and passed for 300. Meredith had to leave the game temporarily after a head-on collision with Wayne Harris. On a two-point try, Lance was stopped a half-dozen times, no chance in the world, but he kept spinning and twisting and somehow got in for a 15-14 lead. SMU gave us a safety and we won, 17-14. That put us in a three-way tie with Texas and TCU for the championship and sent us to the Gator

Bowl. In fact, all our conference wins in '59 were vital in the sense that we either won them in the fourth quarter, or they were so close that we could have lost any of them in the fourth quarter.

Any win over Texas is big, and we have five of those. I've examined the Texas series in detail in another area of this book, so we'll pause here just long enough to emphasize that our 24-23 win at Austin in '60 sent us to the Cotton Bowl (and opened up Texas recruiting to us) and that our 14-13 and 27-24 victories were epics that kept our 22-game winning streak alive in 1964-65.

In a long winning streak, all victories are big, so we have 22 to consider right there. Coming back in the fourth quarter and beating Nebraska in the Cotton Bowl 10-7 gave us the national championship. One might argue that Arkansas never won a more important game than that one.

We had to beat a good Rice team at Little Rock in '60 to win the championship. Wayne Harris stopped Rice at our three-yard line with a late interception, and we drove for a last-minute field goal by Mickey Cissell, 3-0. At Fayetteville in '61, we were trailing A&M by 8-7 in the fourth quarter, back on our 10-yard line facing third-and-10. Alworth got away from three men to launch a halfback pass to Paul Dudley that started us on a winning drive and a final score of 15-8, worth a tie for our third straight championship.

Our national prestige took a considerable leap when our 1968 team defeated a great Georgia squad in the Sugar Bowl, 16-2. We caught the Texas Aggies undefeated and No. 2 in the nation in December of '75, and, when we whipped them soundly in a nationally televised game, we reclaimed the Cotton Bowl after a 10-year absence.

I can't judge which victories meant the most, but I can tell you which defeats hurt the worst. There were three of them: Texas in 1962, 7-3; Louisiana State in the 1966 Cotton Bowl game, 14-7; and Texas in Big Shootout I of 1969, 15-14. The '62 Texas game cost us a perfect season, a fourth straight Southwest Conference championship, and a possible national title. The LSU game ended our 22-game winning streak and cost us a certain national title. The '69 Texas game cost us a national championship, a perfect season, and a conference championship. Well, it cost us more than that. So many things were riding on that game it was unbelievable. In a sense we were playing for the championship of a whole decade, because Ar-

Frank shared "Coach of the Year" honors with Ara Parseghian in 1964.

kansas and Texas had so thoroughly dominated the SWC during the '60s.

In 1965, *Sports Illustrated* featured Razorback wingback Harry Jones on its cover and the cover story was entitled "Arkansas: The New Dynasty." And we were close to a dynasty. So very, very close. During the 1960s, the Razorbacks posted a regular-season record of 80-19-1. The Texas Longhorns went 80-18-2 for those same 10 years. Add the bowl games, and we were 82-24-1 to Texas' 86-19-3. In conference games, the two teams came out of the Big Shootout with exactly the same record for the decade, 55-14-1. Arkansas and Texas each won (or shared) five SWC championships during the '60s.

From November of 1958 until the end of the 1971 season, Arkansas went 112-31-2. At the time of the *Sports Illustrated* article, we had won league championships in '59, '60, '61, and '64, and were about to win another in '65. We missed by a half-game in '62, suffered a "down" year in '63, came back with our national championship team in '64, and another perfect season in '65. So those three losses, all during our peak period, cost us a chance to go up there on a pedestal with few other college football teams in history. We would have been placed in a situation like that of Texas and Alabama; we would have leaped to a point where your recruiting is nearly automatic.

You can't win 'em all; I'm aware of that. I also know it's pointless to agonize over a play or two in a close loss. You don't think about the close games you win—you think of those that deprive you of something special. The Razorbacks won one national championship during the '60s, but it almost was four. We had two perfect seasons, but it almost was four or five.

Our 1966 team lost the Cotton Bowl bid twice in the same day. I have never been able to analyze our 21-16 loss to Texas Tech in any regular football sense because of its tragic prologue—the death of Claud Smithey. Claud was a fifth-year senior from Searcy, married, with an infant daughter. Our team doctors advised him to drop out of football because of a head injury, but he went to a doctor in Louisiana who cleared him to play. Claud was determined to play his senior year. He followed me around all the time. Finally, the week of the Texas A&M game, about three weeks after he obtained a doctor's clearance, we let him go through a few drills.

A&M had a group of talented sophomores, including Edd Hargett, the quarterback who carried the Aggies to the Cotton Bowl the following season. With their 3-0 record, they led us in the league race to that point; we'd been upset by Baylor. Our holdover veterans from the 22-game winning streak saw a real challenge in the Aggies and played a superb game at College Station and won 34-0. That was the night that Jon Brittenum, boxed up against the sideline, shifted hands and completed a lefthanded pass. Claud Smithey went in for four or five plays at the end of the game. In the dressing room right after the game, he lapsed into a coma. I still have cold chills when I think about it; I'd never seen that before. He was taken to a hospital at Houston and never regained consciousness. We studied the game film by the hour, and nowhere could we see a play where Claud's head was jarred in the slightest.

We beat Rice, 31-20, and then won a showdown with SMU, 22-0, on a day David Dickey gave us ball control by carrying 38 times. If we beat Texas Tech, as we were heavily favored to do, we'd do no worse than tie with SMU for the conference championship and receive our third straight Cotton Bowl bid. Early that week, Texas Tech coach J. T. King made some statements that drew headlines all over the Southwest. "Teams that are going to bowls, and have a chance to win championships, get all the breaks in officiating," J. T. said, or something to that effect. His theme was that officials tended unconsciously to protect highly ranked, bowl-bound teams with conference prestige at stake, and so forth. Some reporters called me about it, and I had no comment. But I doublted that we would be "protected" at Lubbock.

About 1:30 the afternoon on Tuesday before the Tech game, I received a call that Claud Smithey had died. I called my minister, talked to him, and started to reflect on what position I should take as the coach. Some on my staff said, "We're playing for the championship—let's don't tell the players until after practice. Let's try to have a good practice." I couldn't do that. "No, we have to tell them," I said. "We're going to discuss it with them and see what they want to do." We told them when they assembled for Tuesday's practice; we had some prayer there together, and the players wanted to go ahead and practice. All the seniors, to a man, wanted to go to the funeral at Searcy on Thursday.

I had to take stock in myself and review again all the things I was doing professionally. What's really important in life? Someone on my staff said, "Let's play this one for Claud." He meant well, but I vetoed it. "No, we're not going to talk about that, either," I said. "We'll play this game because the players want us to play it. We'll go through with it, but we'll take it in an atmosphere of deep sorrow and regret. We'll let it run its course, but we're not going to manufacture any type of cause or slogan."

We went to the funeral on Thursday, and, when we stopped in to visit the family, the minister called me aside. "Coach, the family wants you to say the prayer at the graveside," he said. I wanted to, but I wasn't sure I could. The family was so shocked and so grief-stricken, and it was such an emotional service. I just wasn't sure I could do it. I had a couple of hours' notice and I wrote down some things I wanted to say, but I remember that as I stood at the gravesite, I wasn't sure any sound would come out of my mouth. The words did come out, because I drew strength from somewhere else. I forgot everything I intended to say, but it came out and I got through it somehow.

In defense of our squad, we had six starters out of the Tech game, including our two-time All-American tackle, Loyd Phillips, and Harry Jones, our best breakaway threat. Despite the injuries, despite the fact that we obviously were not sharp in our concentration, we moved the ball, took a 10-7 lead, and were on the verge of shoving across a touchdown that would probably have put the game out of reach.

On two consecutive quarterback sneaks, it appeared to us that Jon Brittenum went across both times, but the two officials on the sides of the formation did not call a touchdown. The two men, Adrian Burk and Lyle Blackwood, had both played for me at Baylor. They didn't see it, and maybe if we didn't get it in far enough for an official to see, we didn't deserve it. Anyway, the Texas Tech Red Raiders took heart, fired themselves up, and beat us. It was their first victory over Arkansas in 10 tries.

We were on our way to the dressing room, broken-hearted, when somebody ran up and said, "Baylor's beating SMU and you're back in the Cotton Bowl." If SMU lost, Arkansas, Texas, and SMU would finish in a three-way tie for first, and the Razorbacks would go because of wins over the other two titleholders. The entire team gathered around a radio, and you never saw a group of youngsters perk up so much. SMU blocked a Baylor kick, however, and won with 15 seconds on the clock. We lost the Cotton Bowl twice in the same day. You talk about feeling drained.

On the plane ride home, we were empty-handed with an 8-2 record. Some of the upperclassmen came by and said, "Coach, let's don't go to a bowl."

"We could go to the Liberty Bowl or the Bluebonnet," I said. "We might even have a chance at the Gator."

"No, we want to stay home."

"Okay, it's up to you," I said. "If you don't want to go, we won't."

A lot of this had to do with Claud's death, and some of it had to do with the disappointment at Lubbock. These seniors had been to two Cotton Bowls and taken part in a 22-game winning streak and a national championship. They'd played for the national championship in the previous Cotton Bowl, and opened the season expecting to do so again. Now, they'd had enough.

We suffered sub-par seasons only twice during the 1960s, both times when we failed to get a quarterback established. The quarterback is such a key figure. All the pressure—the public pressure—ultimately comes to rest on the quarterback and the head coach. I would bet that 90 percent of all of the football talk Barbara ever heard from me somehow involved the quarterback. That's all I talked about at home. Who's gonna be the quarterback? What's the quarterback thinking? Where's our next quarterback coming from? This went on for 30 years.

When we attended Jim Mackenzie's funeral, Barbara said, "Frank, I'm embarrassed to tell you what I'm thinking." Well, that got my curiosity, and I asked, "What is it, Barbara?" She said, "No I'm not going to tell you." I kept insisting, and finally she said, "I just looked at the casket, and I thought, 'Jim, you don't have to worry about recruiting a quarterback.'"

James Monroe could walk through the defense for more yards than any quarterback I ever saw. He was the best signal-caller. He led us to the first championship, in '59, even though he hurt his arm that year. He's an engineer now.

George McKinney and Billy Moore competed for two years. In all my career, this was the only time I used a two-quarterback system—just run 'em in and out, play 'em equally, and try to guess who's got the best chance in certain situations. Billy would get hurt and George would play more, and George would get hurt and Billy would play more. The system was right for these two. We won in '60 and '61 with them, and then Billy had another year, and he made All-American in '62. McKinney was a competitor. He couldn't throw and couldn't run, but somehow he did both and won for you. Billy Moore was the most exciting runner at quarterback that I can ever remember. He was so quick—like a hiccup, some said—and a fair passer his last two years. He wanted to do it himself. General Neyland had an old saying at Tennessee: "If your quarterback takes over on third down and makes it, you'll have a good team. If he has to rely on somebody else, you will be average or worse."

We recruited Billy with our first freshman group, but I had no idea what kind of a football player he was. At one point, I tried to talk him into transferring to another school; I even offered to help him

Billy Moore

Jon Brittenum

James Monroe

Scott Bull

George McKinney

Bill Montgomery

Joe Ferguson

Arkansas had great quarterbacks during the Broyles years.

get a football scholarship somewhere else. Not because he "hit a professor," but because I was afraid he'd never be more than a marginal player with us, and I knew his pride demanded more. Boy, was I fooled.

I should explain that the "professor" Billy "hit" was a young man who had a teaching assistantship, and the altercation had nothing to do with the classroom. As I understand it, some of our players were helping someone push a stalled car on an icy street. The car they were pushing then struck another car. An argument followed, and before it was over, Billy "hit a professor." That indicting phrase attached itself to the incident, and never let go.

Pete Raney and others who knew Billy urged him to stay at Arkansas during that time when he might have left. They didn't realize how good a football player he was either, but they knew he was a winner. One of the main regrets of my whole coaching career was that I stuck Billy back into a game against Texas Tech to try to break a school scoring record. He hurt his knee and couldn't go against Ole Miss in the Sugar Bowl a few weeks later, and that taught me a lesson. Always protect your players. Let individual records take care of themselves. When the game is won, get your regulars out of there and keep them out.

Fred Marshall was strong-legged: a better runner than we thought, a better passer than we thought; an outstanding leader. Jon Brittenum was the best passer on the move that I've ever seen. He could throw it like a frozen rope on the sprint-out series. He was the perfect passer-runner for the system we played at the time. He was quick and had a rifle arm. Jon had a tough time early. He was highly recruited, and everybody in his home state was counting on him to be great right away, but it took time—as it usually does. He played as a sophomore while we were in that revolving situation with Marshall and Brittenum and Billy Gray in '63.

Jon started against Texas' national championship team that year, and played well. We lost by 17-13 and had a chance to win it in the last three minutes. Jon lost his confidence toward the end of the year, with the team losing, and I called him in after the season and told him he'd be redshirted. He came back and was, of course, our quarterback on the second 10-0 team in '65, and the near-championship team in '66.

In 1967 we couldn't make up our minds over Ronny South or

John Eichler. We didn't show any confidence in them and kept switching. It turned out to be another bad year like '63.

Bill Montgomery knew more football than any quarterback I had ever seen at that time. He was intelligent; he could have called the plays as well as, if not better than, our coaches. He knew that much football, and he had the instinctive feel for the situation down there on the field. We went 28-5 the three years Bill played. We lost to Texas three times while the Longhorns were winning 30 games in a row. We also lost to Archie Manning and Ole Miss in the Sugar Bowl. And we lost to Stanford and Jim Plunkett. Three of those losses— Texas in Big Shootout I at the end of '69, Ole Miss in the Sugar Bowl, and Stanford in the '70 opener—came consecutively, all on national TV, and were all thrillers: 15-14, 27-22, and 34-28. We were that close, and Bill had some of his greatest days in those three heart-breakers.

The state of Texas contained eight major quarterback prospects in 1967, and from the beginning we knew Montgomery was the one we should go after. We were in the process of shifting to what was known as the Florida State offense. Don Breaux joined us from Florida State and we added our I-formation to what they did and, when we mixed it all together, we had everything: two wide-outs, dropback passes with pro techniques, the veer option, the counter option, the old split-T (or down-the-line) option, the bread-and-butter work by the tailback, and all types of roll-outs, sprint-outs and keepers for the quarterback. Breaux, Mervin Johnson, and Richard Williamson formed a superior offensive staff in coaching that system, and Montgomery was the perfect player to make it work. We were known as a passing team, but we actually threw fewer passes per number of plays than we did a couple of years earlier when we were known as a running team. The threat of the pass opened up running and gave us the ideal balance.

Barbara took part in the recruiting of only two players. One was Lance Alworth and the other was Bill Montgomery. Johnny Majors, before he left for Iowa State, did most of the recruiting of Montgomery, but Barbara went down and visited their home.

"If you get Bill Montgomery," we'd hear around Dallas, "you've got yourself another coach." The reference was to Bill's father, Carl "Catfish" Montgomery. I never found any justification for that. I admired and became very fond of Catfish. He loved that boy, he loved his family, and I don't fault anyone for being proud of his children. He was proud of all the Razorbacks and was a great cheerleader for us, no question about it. He never embarrassed me, and he never interfered in any way. We had peak years with Bill in 1968-69-70. He could run, throw, think, and lead.

Joe Ferguson was probably the most intense youngster that I've ever seen play. I never saw anybody who worked harder, or was more a perfectionist, than Ferguson. Everybody wanted him, and we didn't think we had a chance, but his high school coach at Shreveport, Louisiana, liked our offense and believed Joe could run it well.

I don't guess we ever knew a more giddy and exciting period than the early months of 1969. We started the year with our young team knocking off Georgia in the Sugar Bowl, raising the possibility we could win the national championship that year. ABC-TV studied the teams and the schedules and concluded that the Arkansas-Texas game was the best bet to settle the national title in the centennial season of college football. ABC asked us and Texas to shift our game at Fayetteville to December, with the gamble that it would indeed be the No. 1 game.

In the middle of all this, we signed Joe Ferguson, who'd been a regional legend since his junior year in high school. At the signing ceremony at Shreveport, I was quoted as saying, essentially, that Joe Ferguson meant a national championship. Actually, I said that any team with a quarterback of Joe Ferguson's caliber should certainly have a chance to win a national championship before he graduated.

Our fans saw what a great passer Joe was while he was on the freshman team in '69, and then in '70, Bill Montgomery's senior year, they'd holler for Joe each time Bill made a mistake. This wasn't in Joe's best interests, and it certainly wasn't in Bill's best interests. Back in spring practice, people were saying, "Well, Ferguson's gonna beat out Montgomery." It wasn't any part of Joe's doing; it was just idle talk by fans who were captivated by this exciting newcomer.

We fell behind Stanford, 24-0, in the first game of Joe's sophomore year. We sent him in and he completed some passes and moved us close, and then we brought Montgomery back to hand the ball off and run the option play and try to get it in. Some people in the stands didn't understand and they booed—booed the decision, not Montgomery—but that was terrible for him to hear. Everything was

". . . we signed Joe Ferguson, who'd been a regional legend since his junior year in high school."

soon in proper perspective. Bill had a remarkable senior year, de- spite some injuries, and Joe had a lot of playing time when games were put away. He looked super. Zip! Zip! Zip! Right down the field.

By the time Joe took over in 1971, our squad was not as deep, strong, and experienced as it had been, and we didn't have the of- fensive line or the running backs we needed around a passer like Joe. He still had a great junior year. He ripped Texas apart in the rain at Little Rock, 31-7, and we missed the Cotton Bowl because of a 17-9 loss to A&M or a 24-24 tie with Rice: Take your pick. With nothing to fear from the running attack except Dickey Morton on the sprint draw, opponents kept Joe looking into defensive schemes that rushed three, and defended the pass with eight. We simply didn't have the material to complement him. Like most teams that can pass but can't run, we went through some dizzy highs and lows.

Then Don Breaux left. Its hard for a kid, when his coach leaves, particularly when the quarterback and the coach are as close as Joe and Don were. Joe was broken-hearted. He tried to make the best of the situation and so did Richard Williamson, who replaced Don. Boy, it was tough in '72. We no longer had the material to run the offense that could take advantage of Joe's ability. We changed to the wishbone in the middle of the year (we'd been running it on goal-line and short-yardage since '71), and we didn't do any better with it than the passing game. For the last game against Texas Tech we used Scott Bull and didn't play Joe. That was the toughest decision I ever had to make and I hated it for Joe's sake, but we were going to run option plays and do the things we planned to do the next year with Bull. To no one's surprise, Joe became an outstanding pro quarterback for Buffalo. I wish our squad had been stronger and more stable when he was with us, because he certainly would have had a fabulous career. He was such a fine, dedicated youngster and such a great passer.

The next two years, 1973-74, we had a revolving situation with three fine young men, Scott Bull, Mike Kirkland, and Mark Miller. Each time it seemed one of them was on the verge of coming into his own, an injury or something intervened. We had our weakest and least experienced squad in '73, and we were always changing, always groping. Finally, we put it all together again in '75, with Scott Bull at quarterback. Scott was one of those winners who defy easy classification, like George McKinney and Pepper Rodgers. I can't explain it, but under some quarterbacks every man on the team plays 15 percent better, and when everybody on a good team plays 15 percent better, well, you've got quite a thing going for you. Scott shook off a terribly discouraging game against Texas in midseason, shook off the public criticism that fell on him, and led us to the Cotton Bowl.

My last quarterback, Ron Calcagni, became a great player for Lou Holtz in his junior and senior years. You could see the elements of all our other winning quarterbacks in Ron, although I believe each quarterback is a unique individual in a unique situation, and to compare them is pointless and unfair. I still believe we would have won in '76 if Ron, then a sophomore, hadn't been injured.

On the subject of quarterbacks, George Cole used to tell a story about the old days when a Razorback team was trying to make up its mind among three of them in the spring. No one would come to the front. They all seemed about the same. A booster asked

George about the quarterback situation, and George didn't paint a very rosy picture.

"But you've got three of them," the man said. "All just alike."

"Exactly," George said. "And don't you know you're in trouble when you can't tell somebody who your quarterback is?"

That will remain true forever.

13
THE POOCH KICK,
AND OTHER MISHAPS

Will I ever live down the pooch kick? Unless you are a deep, dyed-in-the-wool Arkansas fan of long standing, you probably don't even know what I'm talking about. If you are, you are probably laughing or griping all over again.

The pooch kick incident happened October 8, 1966, at Fayetteville in a Baylor game that broke our 16-game winning streak in the Southwest Conference and handed us our first regular-season loss in nearly three years.

When the rules came in that the kicking team could "down" a punt inside the opponents' 10-yard line, a new wrinkle appeared in field position strategy. When a team stalled on its opponents' side of the field, it could kick the ball straight up (or "pooch" it) and let the linemen try to down the ball close to the goal.

I've said all along, when you get shut out, it's your defense that keeps you from scoring and when you score a lot of points, it's also your defense that gave you the scoring opportunities. When the ball is on your opponents' 20-yard line, they are 80 yards from scoring and your team is 20 yards from scoring—no matter who has possession of the ball. You should score more often than they do.

Baylor made very little yardage against us that afternoon, and we had marched up and down the field all through a scoreless tie. Terry Southall, the Baylor quarterback, had a sensational day punting the football. He kept kicking us back to our 15 or 20, and we'd zip to a few first downs, make a mistake or two, and give up the ball without scoring. In the middle of the fourth quarter, we faced a fourth-and-three at the Baylor 29. A sprinkling rain was falling. We debated on

John Bridger's Baylor Bears always gave the Razorbacks a lot of trouble.

the sideline. Most coaches would agree that the greatest shift in momentum in a football game takes place when a team is stopped on fourth down, especially late in the game when the team that is about to lose the game suddenly sees a chance to win it. Baylor hadn't been able to do anything offensively. We decided we'd pooch kick the ball on fourth-and-three. We'd push them back inside their 10, force a punt, and take another crack at a touchdown or field goal.

This was the only time in all my coaching that I ever elected to punt that close to the other team's goal. The center snapped the ball over the head of our punter, Martine Bercher, and Baylor recovered at midfield. Now, *there* was a shift in momentum. Baylor scored on three Southall passes, the last one a 27-yarder to Bobby Green. We were behind, 7-0, and we lost by that score, although we did come back with a touchdown pass that was nullified because a lineman was downfield. Maybe he was six inches downfield.

On my TV show the next day, I tried to explain the advantages of the pooch kick. That's when people started the slogan: "Deliver me from the pooch kick." I'm afraid the pooch kick is fated to live on forever in Arkansas infamy—like the Ole Miss game of 1960 and the Liberty Bowl game of 1971. That night at Little Rock, October 22, 1960, we played a tremendous defensive game against an outstanding squad of well-coached athletes. We led, 7-0, until a breakdown in the secondary let them hit a bomb for a 7-7 tie. As time ran out in the fourth quarter, the Rebels put on a desperation drive to within field-goal range. Arkansas fans were counting down the seconds. "NINE, EIGHT, SEVEN. . . ." I don't remember anything unusual about the crowd noise, and, anyway, on a field-goal attempt, there aren't any "audibles" or snap-count adjustments at the line of scrimmage to be obscured by crowd noise. In any event, the referee, Tommy Bell, of the Southeastern Conference (and later one of the top officials in the National Football League), waved his hands to stop the clock with three seconds left.

Our players saw him, and relaxed. The Mississippi players, with their backs to him, didn't see him signal for time. The center snapped the ball, the holder put it down, and Allen Green kicked it. Perfectly. Split the uprights, as they say. Time was out, though, so they had to kick it again. Then Bell had to make a decision to start the clock when the ball was ready for play, or start the clock on the snap—which he decided to do. Here is what you can see in the film: When Green hit the ball the second time, and missed it to the left, he started kicking the ground in dejection. Our players were jumping for joy. The film shows starkly that their players thought it went wide, and our players thought it went wide. Everybody sitting in the end zone that night thought it missed by six to eight feet.

As soon as Green kicked the ball, Bell's hands went up for "good" and then he ran off the field. Fans came boiling down on the field, fights broke out, and several minutes passed before some of our players knew we lost, 10-7. I don't know how many people those end zone seats in War Memorial Stadium held, but it seems as though

"I almost never went after the officials, but this time I did."

every person in Arkansas was down there with the perfect angle to see Green's kick go wide. For the next year, or maybe the next five years, you could say "Thomas P. Bell" anywhere in the state of Arkansas and open it all up again (Thomas P. Bell was the referee's listing in the game program).

When we were matched with Tennessee in the '71 Liberty Bowl, we had a big squabble with the Southeastern Conference office because I didn't want Georgia Tech grads in the ball game. The three Southeastern Conference officials originally assigned were men I'd coached at Tech, or who had been my teammates there. I didn't think that was good at all; it placed undue pressure on them. I argued and argued, and finally the SEC agreed to take them off. Instead, they assigned, as I recall, three Tennessee residents. I'd known the SEC supervisor of officials, George Gardner, a long time and I respected him, but in this case, he was just plain hard-headed. One of the SEC assignees was Preston Watts of Memphis, a name Arkansas fans identify as readily as Thomas P. Bell.

We played a superb game against a good Tennessee team and led, 13-7, when Bill McClard lined up for a 48-yard field goal try. He kicked it and the scoreboard read "16-7" a few seconds before the field goal was disallowed. Watts, the field judge, had called a holding penalty. In the technique of protecting for field goals, you don't use your hands. You use your body. You take an inside step and everybody turns to the inside and shields the kicker and holder like a cup—like a V formation, with the kicker behind the V. You just don't use your hands.

The next possession, we called a delayed screen pass from Joe Ferguson to Jon Richardson, which had been very successful for us. Richardson was knocked loose from the football right in front of the Tennessee bench. The Vols in those days were known for trying to influence officials and spectators on a fumble. All their players would automatically leap up and start pointing their way. I'm not critical of that; I'm just saying they did a magnificent job of convincing everybody in the stadium that every loose ball was theirs.

We recovered the football. Tom Reed handed the ball to the referee, MacDuff Simpson, of the Southwest Conference. There must have been nearly 22 players on the pile-up. The ball hit the ground, and then it was just thud, thud, thud, thud as player after player went down in the scramble. Unwinding the pile took a very long time, and Reed got up with the ball. In fact, Tennessee players later told our players they never had the ball. All this time, Watts signalled "Tennessee's ball." He contended a Tennessee player had the ball and that it was taken away by Arkansas. It was my argument that the referee should have overruled Watts. It was also my argument that Tennessee officials shouldn't have been assigned to the game in the first place. Tennessee scored with less than two minutes left, and beat us 14-13.

Not long after this incident, all bowls except the Rose started bringing in neutral officiating crews as a matter of course. The Southwest Conference finally acknowledged in 1979 the merit of the University of Arkansas's contention that "outside" officials should be used in certain SWC games involving Arkansas.

The list of Southwest Conference officials includes a handful of Arkansas residents, none of whom ever work U of A football games.

Can you imagine the uproar that would come the way of an Arkansas resident who threw a flag against Arkansas on a critical down? Of course you can. They understand that in Texas, too, but they had never noticed the corollary; Arkansas, for generations, has played in a Texas league with Texas-based game officials. I don't mean to belabor the point; I don't question the dedication or basic integrity of game officials. I'm talking about human nature and common sense.

We tend to forget the questionable (or just plain wrong) calls that fall our way. Part of the breaks, we figure. The most embarrassing call that favored us came in our Iowa State game in 1973. We scored a touchdown with a 12-man offensive unit. Photographs show us with a full-house backfield plus a flanker. We were in the wishbone with an unbalanced line a lot during that game, but on this particular down, we were in a wishbone and a slot-I as well. The substitute didn't come out, and I didn't catch it. Neither did the officials. My coaches were afraid to tell me anything about it until the end of the game. Finally, Mervin Johnson explained. I didn't know what Earle Bruce, the Iowa State coach, was yelling about at the time. Of course, he'd been told by his coaches upstairs that we had too many men on the field.

I apologized at the end of the game, but I didn't know what to do. The weakside end who stayed in had nothing to do with the play. We won the game, 21-19. The 12-man touchdown was an innocent mistake on our part, and I regret that it happened that way. The officials should have caught it, but they're like coaches and players. They're human, too.

14
CLOUT AT THE POLLS

When I first came to Arkansas, one of the first things John Barn-hill did was to issue a stern warning about politics. "Frank, I want to give you what I think is good, sound advice," he said. "Don't ever get involved in politics. When there's an election, you try to arrange to be out of the state so there's no chance you might involve the school and the football team in anything political."

I lived up to that. I did exactly what he told me, with one exception. Well, there were two exceptions actually, but one doesn't count. I appeared at a rally at Little Rock on behalf of an education bond issue, but only because I was told to do so by the Board of Trustees. I made it clear that I was requested to appear, and left as soon as I finished speaking.

I couldn't see any harm, though, in supporting a new regional airport to serve the Fayetteville-Springdale-Rogers area. The jets won't land at Drake Field in Fayetteville. For the Razorbacks going out, or visiting teams coming in, that means flying to Fort Smith, changing planes, flying back to Fort Smith and changing planes, again. An election was set in 1969, for Washington and Benton counties to combine their taxes for a new airport at Tonitown, a community adjacent to Fayetteville that several generations of football fans know well for its restaurants. Everyone anticipated the measure would pass. There was tremendous opposition from farmers, however, who contended that their hens would not lay eggs, and their cows would not give milk, because of the jet noise. No one really paid much attention, and the proposal's backers were shocked when they lost the election by about 400 votes.

The business leaders were aghast. They had to have a regional airport. A new election was called. Some of my friends came to me and said, "Frank, can you help us? You can swing the 400 votes."

"I'll help you," I said.

This was a few weeks before Big Shootout I with Texas. Interest in the Razorbacks is always at a fever pitch in Arkansas, but this season was far more feverish than normal. We'd won 14 or 15 in a row, and it was obvious our Texas game would settle the national championship.

We set up little town meetings each Wednesday and Thursday night for three weeks leading up to the election. I'd go into four or five communities and make an appeal. I'd quote Darrell and other visiting coaches, and I really turned loose all the celebrated Broyles salesmanship. I'd give away 10 autographed footballs for lucky-number drawings. Crowds overflowed the high school gyms and I never faced warmer or more responsive audiences in my life.

We lost the election. Not by 400 votes this time, though. We lost by 4000.

An old retired newspaperman at Rogers, producing his anti-airport newspaper out of his own home, panned me as "The Football Coach," a meddling city slicker from the seething metropolis of Fayetteville, who wanted to impose all this jet racket on everybody's milk and egg production. I read his stuff and felt like laughing and crying at the same time. He really took me to task.

We still don't have a new airport. We lost two subsequent elections, but I didn't involve myself in those in any way. And I never will again. Even a city slicker can tell the difference between 400 and 4000. At least, this one can.

15
MY FRIEND DARRELL ROYAL

Darrell Royal and I became close friends and remained so through 19 Arkansas-Texas football games, and beyond. That fact might represent a larger upset than anything that ever happened on a football field. As far as I know, our relationship is unprecedented in such an intense rivalry. Each year the week of the Arkansas-Texas game, we shut off communication for a few days. Otherwise, we visited back and forth on the phone all the time and spent as much leisure time together as possible.

We talked football, of course, but we never discussed or debated specifics of Arkansas-Texas games until after we retired together in 1976. It wasn't until then that I realized Darrell considered Texas' 27-24 loss to Arkansas in 1965 the most disappointing and damaging defeat of his career. It wasn't until then that he knew the magnitude of my disappointment in the '62 and '69 games.

In all those coaching years we had two firm but unspoken agreements: That we would never talk football on a golf course and never discuss our own games, period. This lasted until shortly after we retired. At that time we went to Bo Schembechler's coaching clinic at Michigan, and, during the plane ride home, Darrell said, "Frank, its all over now and I don't care, but were you picking up our signals from the bench in '71?"

"That's the first time you ever asked a question about something that happened in one of our games," I said. "Were you picking up our signals in the '62 game?" Since then, we've gone at it in this vein for hours, but still, never on the golf course.

When Texas suffered its third straight 6-4 season in 1967, and there was negative speculation about which way the UT program was headed, a writer asked me what I thought about it. "Darrell Royal will retire some day with one of the greatest coaching records in the history of football," I said. The next year he went to the wishbone and Texas ultimately made six straight Cotton Bowl trips, and had a 30-game winning streak. And really, I don't think Darrell ever thought of himself as a great coach. Acclaim and success never swelled his head or tampered with his personality. When he was on top of the world at Texas, he was essentially the same man I'd first known as a struggling young coach at Mississippi State. When he lost to Baylor for the first time in 1974, I dropped him a note and told him he had no peer in our generation of coaches. I knew he'd be feeling low at that point, and I had never forgotten how much I appreciated a thoughtful note from Ara Parseghian after LSU broke our 22-game winning streak.

Darrell and I are not much alike in personality; we both agree to that. Our wives, Edith and Barbara, are very much alike and very compatible. As the years grew, we were together more and more often in the summers. A pattern evolved. Edith and Barbara would shop and sight-see together while Darrell and I went to the golf course. We'd play golf all day and they'd spend our money. Aside from golf, Darrell and I have little in common when it comes to seeking out entertainment or recreation. Darrell enjoys the Las Vegas scene; I wouldn't give you a nickel for Las Vegas. Darrell is famous for his love of "picking" and I still enjoy dancing to Glenn Miller. A few years ago, at one of our coaches' golf tournaments at Hot Springs, one of Darrell's picking friends kept everybody enthralled until near sunrise. At the time, few had ever heard of him. About a year later, everybody knew his name—Willie Nelson.

Well, I like Willie Nelson's music (it would be almost un-American not to) and I don't dislike picking in general, but I still prefer the big-band music that was standard when Barbara and I were dating: Glenn Miller, Tommy and Jimmy Dorsey, Harry James. Country singers gave Darrell an extra outlet from his coaching. He's known all the great ones personally, and they have tremendous love and respect for him. I think Barbara summed it up accurately when she said Darrell learned to show affection for other people from his picking friends.

"The four of us spend a lot of time together."

Although we are opposite in many respects, Darrell and I found early that we shared the same principles and philosophies of coaching. We are about the same age and we arrived in the league about the same time. (He took over at Texas in 1957 and I came to Arkansas a year later.) I'll always be grateful for the pep talk he gave me on the field at Austin when I was completely despondent about our program in '58.

The second time our teams met, in War Memorial Stadium at Little Rock in 1959, we cut a pattern that lasted more than a decade: Arkansas and Texas, fighting it out for conference titles and possible national titles in classic games of razor-thin desperation. Texas won the '59 game, 13-12. This was the night James Monroe took the Razorbacks on an 89-yard, 19-play drive off the second-half kickoff. No big gainers and no mistakes. We just inched our way along for nearly 10 minutes, and Monroe scored a touchdown on a keeper from the three that gave us a 12-7 lead. Lance Alworth fumbled a punt, and Texas recovered at our 31. The Longhorns won it on a left-handed halfback pass from Bart Shirley to Jack Collins—a play that officially covered only three yards.

TCU knocked off Texas later and the Razorbacks, the Horns, and Frogs wound up in a three-way tie for the championship. No one could tell it at the time, but that was a torch-passing year in the Southwest Conference. The tri-championship represented a last hurrah for Abe Martin's TCU teams, which had been dominant for about five years, and touched off a Texas-Arkansas era that would prevail through the 1960s.

In 1960, we went into the Texas game facing elimination from the conference race. We had just been soundly beaten by one of John Bridger's best Baylor teams. The score was 28-14 but it wasn't that close. Baylor ran a pro offense that we didn't see otherwise, and we made the mistake of assuming a passing team couldn't or wouldn't run. We guarded against the pass while Baylor ran us to death with Ronnie Bull. It was a painful but valuable lesson. By the time we adjusted, we were out of the ball game. The next week we went to Austin for a regional television game.

That Saturday morning at the pre-game meal, our players sat around and read an Austin sportswriter's opinion that the Baylor game proved that Arkansas was not of championship caliber. Our players had a lot of pride, and this article got their blood boiling. The result was that Texas led us by 14-0 and 23-14 that afternoon, but the Razorbacks won, 24-23. We kept coming back with great passes by George McKinney and great catches by Jimmy Collier. We finally moved as close as 23-21 when Texas over-reacted to Collier and Alworth on one side, and McKinney came back the other way with a short pass to Jarrell Williams, who ran it in from the 19. Late in the fourth quarter, we secured field position when we bottled Texas up and Harold Horton's 15-yard punt return set us up at midfield.

Mickey Cissell, a substitute fullback, was our place-kicker. Back in September, Mickey had wanted to quit football. I'd told him he wasn't going to quit. "We don't have another kicker," I told him. "And you're not going to let this team down, you're not going to let yourself down. You're going to stay here and kick for this football team. If you walk out that door, you're going to have to walk over my body and whip me. If you get out of town, I'll have a police car after you. You are not going to quit."

At Austin, we just hoped we could get close enough to give Mickey a shot at it in the final minute. On fourth down and two at the 20, Alworth dived for a first down that had to be measured. Darrell always thought the Longhorns had Lance stopped. "You talk about lucky breaks," he said to me not long ago. "I remember the head linesman spotted the ball on Lance's run where he didn't make a first down. Then the umpire (who's not supposed to do the spotting) came and grabbed it, moved it forward, and you got the first down by maybe a half-inch."

"Darrell," I said, "the official who made that spot just happened to be one of your teammates in college."

We made the first down over to the side, at a bad kicking angle. We had two time-outs left. We used one of them to decide we could risk McKinney running one more time to try and place the ball in the middle of the field. George kept off-tackle and fell for six yards to the 12. We called our last time-out with just a few seconds to play. The wind had shifted a few minutes before, and now it was behind us as Cissell went out to try the field goal. Mickey kicked it as hard as he could. It came down like a dying dove, hit the goal post, and bounced in.

Everybody cried in the dressing room. Beating Texas was something special. Everybody was still crying when we got on the plane to go home. Several thousand people waited to meet us, and, when our DC-3 touched down at Fayetteville, some of the students ran right out on the airstrip and for a few seconds we were afraid some of them were going to run right into the propellers. We won the conference championship outright, with Cissell kicking another last-minute field goal that beat Rice 3-0. For the first time, the Razorbacks had won league titles back to back.

Our chances of making it three in a row didn't look too hot the following October when Texas beat us at Fayetteville, 33-7. The 1961 Longhorns were especially deep in good backs (James Saxton, Mike Cotten, Ray Poage, Jack Collins, Jerry Allen Cook, and a terrific sophomore, Tommy Ford), and they were tearing everybody apart out of the flip-flop winged-T. We had to try to contain them with a patchwork defensive unit—our linebackers, Dean Garrett and Tommy Brasher, were hurt, and so were one or two other regulars—and we couldn't keep it close. Texas looked like a national champion most of that season, until TCU upset the Longhorns at Austin in November, 6-0, on a bomb from Sonny Gibbs to Buddy Iles off the hand-back pass. We swept our November schedule and finished in a first-place tie with Texas. Three straight titles.

In 1962, with the most gifted overall squad we'd had to that point, we appropriated the basic features of Darrell's flip-flop offense. We also decided to utilize as many players as possible under the limited substitution rules with a three-platoon system similar to the one Paul Dietzel of LSU pioneered with his undefeated "Chinese Bandits" team of 1958. Under the rules then in effect, a player could enter a game only once a quarter, except for one "wild card" per down. We, and almost every other team, used the wild card to replace a quarterback with a defensive specialist or an offensive center with a linebacker. In 1961, for example, we played Lance Alworth and Paul Dudley at halfbacks on offense, with Darrell Williams and Harold Horton in there most of the time on defense. But we couldn't make wholesale moves when the ball changed hands; specialists had to get in and out one at a time. Offensive players still had to play some defense, and vice versa. In the spring of '62, though, we settled on a No. 1 unit of our best and most experienced all-round players, and two alternate units, mostly sopomores, one primarily for defensive situations and one primarily for offense. I still think, for morale purposes, there has never been a better system. About 35 players really got to play each week.

All that spring and summer, we worried about a fullback. To win big, or maybe win at all, you must have a power-running fullback to punish people inside and keep the defenses honest. We saw no such runner on our squad. Then, deep in the summer, I had an idea.

"Didn't Brabham play fullback in high school?" I asked some of the assistant coaches. "Yes, Coach, he did," one of them said. They all laughed.

Danny Brabham, who came from a small high school at Greensburg, Louisiana, had intended to play football at Tulane and study engineering. The dean of the engineering school at Tulane wrote and warned him that he couldn't play football and major in engineering; he'd have to take his choice. Danny's high school coach got in touch with us, and Jim Mackenzie went down and talked to Danny and signed him. All this happened in August of 1959. I'll never forget how impressed I was when I first saw him. In those days a 6-4, 220-pound fullback was a giant. We put him at linebacker immediately. He did an adequate job as a guard and linebacker a couple of years, and, coming up to his senior year in '62, we were toying around with the possibility of trying him at defensive tackle. But . . . fullback?

I wrote for some of his high school films, and we looked at them for hours. My coaches said, "There's no way." When two-a-day practices started, however, we were in a goal-line scrimmage one day. We stuck Danny in at fullback against a gap-eight defense manned by our best defensive people. He left a trail of bodies the first time he carried the ball. I can still see him against TCU, breaking about 50 yards for a touchdown with that wild stride, those long legs churning. "He's all elbows, knee-bones, and shoe leather," Wilson Matthews said.

This was the most radical personnel move I ever made as a coach, switching a senior linebacker-guard to offensive fullback, yet it was the crowning touch to a great offensive unit. Quarterback Billy Moore could turn the corners at a rate that would give him the conference championship in rushing, Brabham could smash away inside, and they were augmented by a steady tailback, Jesse Branch, and a gifted sophomore wingback, George Rhea Walker, whose career would end prematurely because of injuries.

The Razorbacks went out that fall and demolished Oklahoma State, 34-7; Tulsa, 42-14; and TCU, 42-14. In the middle of the second quarter, we held a 28-0 lead over Baylor. Fans and coaches were shaking their heads and wondering if this wasn't too good to be true. About that time, quarterback Don Trull started hitting passes all over the field, and Baylor began to roll. We spent the rest of that afternoon salvaging a hard-earned 28-21 win. At some point during the wild Baylor comeback, I yelled at our defensive coaches, "I don't want them to make another yard, do you understand? Not another inch!"

Then we moved on to an Arkansas-Texas game in Austin that commanded national attention and a Memorial Stadium sellout crowd of about 65,000. In case you don't know, I'll spare you the suspense. After our defensive unit dominated the game more than three quarters, Texas spent nearly 10 minutes driving 85 yards for a touchdown that beat Arkansas, 7-3. It was maddening. Stan Sparks intercepted a pass that would have stopped the drive, but he was ruled out of bounds. Even Darrell has said that if the play happened on our side of the field, it probably would have stood as an interception. Texas made three measured first downs by maybe a total of three inches and Tommy Ford scored from the four with 36 seconds left. The stands were bedlam all through that long drive, and the cannon that Texas students normally fired for touchdowns blasted with each first down. It was the most agonizing defeat I ever suffered. If I had been on top of the stadium instead of the field, I might have jumped.

We had led, 3-0, since Tom McKnelly's 42-yard field goal in the second quarter. Late in the third quarter, we almost opened it up to 10-0. Texas didn't really threaten until the final drive. One of the most controversial plays in Arkansas history took place after we made a first down at the Texas five in the third period. Doug Dickey was calling the plays upstairs. He asked, "How is Brabham?" because he knew Danny had some hurt ribs. "He can block, but he can't get hit in the ribs," we told him. "Don't give him the ball." On the goal-line, though, Doug studied the Texas defense and thought the call had to go to the fullback. The hole was there, but just as Danny was crossing the goal, he was hit by two great Texas linebackers, Leon Treadwell and Pat Culpepper. The ball flew out, and was recovered by Texas in the end zone. Had Brabham crossed the plane before he fumbled? We thought so, but Texas took over on its 20-yard line.

We didn't lose again that season, and Texas' only blemish was a tie with Rice. We missed the championship by a half-game.

In 1963 the Razorbacks were pre-season favorites in the Southwest Conference because we had so many lettermen who had played as sophomores on our alternate units the year before. The substitution rule had been changed again, however, and the three-team system was no longer feasible. Moreover, we had quarterback problems and we struggled through a 5-5 season. Texas, with 16 or 17 superb all-purpose players, won a national championship. Though we competed strongly the night we met the Longhorns at Little Rock, we still lost by 17-13.

Texas scored on its first three possessions and led 17-0 before Jackie Brasuell's 89-yard kickoff return to the Longhorns' six-yard line put some fire in us. Quarterback Jon Brittenum, then a natural sophomore who was having trouble putting it all together, started against Texas and played well. In fact, he took us on a 90-yard drive. We were in Texas territory with a chance to win in the last three minutes, but we couldn't make it.

One of the big shootouts. Arkansas won this one 27-24 on national TV.

When we met the Longhorns at Austin a year later, Texas hadn't lost a regular-season game in nearly three years, or since the 6-0 upset by TCU in November of 1961. We were 4-0 but we hadn't impressed many people beating Oklahoma State 14-10, an exceptionally good Tulsa team 31-22, TCU 29-6, and Baylor 17-6. Texas was rated No. 1 and looked like a good bet to repeat as national champion. This was the same setting and almost the identical situation we had faced two years earlier at Austin. This one had a different ending, though.

It's funny how a person's mind turns into a brief highlights film as time goes by. If you were in Memorial Stadium on the night of October 17, 1964, chances are you still see Ken Hatfield fleeing 81 yards with a punt return for our first touchdown, and Bobby Crockett catching a 34-yarder from Fred Marshall for our second. You can probably still see Jim Finch in the face of Texas quarterback Marvin Kristynik as he threw for Hix Green on the two-point conversion try at the end. Maybe you still know exactly the spot on the field where the conversion pass fell incomplete, leaving Arkansas the winner by 14-13.

Chances are you have forgotten what a remarkable kicking duel it was between Bobby Nix and Texas' big Ernie Koy. Chances are you don't remember that Texas had 12 men on the field for an Arkansas punting situation, and that gave us a first down and kept us going toward Crockett's touchdown. Chances are you don't remember Texas' early momentum, which reached our 20 before Ronnie Mac Smith defused it by blitzing Kristynik for a 10-yard loss. With time running out in the fourth quarter, Texas was trailing 14-7 and driving 1962-style. When the Longhorns scored and cut it to 14-13, we knew they were going for two points. The only question was how.

Let's go back to 1962 for just a second. Texas was down inside our five, trailing by 3-0 and facing third down. I learned later that Darrell decided to run Tommy Ford off tackle and set the ball right up between the goal posts and kick for a 3-3 tie instead of gambling on a fourth-down run. They called time out and debated. And debated and debated. Darrell took out Ford, who was not a good pass receiver, and replaced him with a halfback who was known to be a good receiver. This was about halfway through the time-out. We figured that meant they were going for two passes, or one pass and a field goal. We called our defense to get into a defend-against-a-pass set, which we called a 4-3 at that time. Just before the ball was snapped, Darrell pulled the halfback we figured as a pass receiver, and sent Ford back in. We knew immediately he has going to run the football. We kept trying to signal our linebackers, Ronnie Caveness and Tommy Brasher, but with all the noise we couldn't get their attention. Ford ran the ball off tackle, scored, and beat us, 7-3. I'm not sure we could have stopped them if we'd been in any other defense, but I like to think we'd have had a better chance.

Now, back to 1964. Texas had scored with a few seconds left, and they were were taking a time-out to decide what play they'd use to go for two points. I grabbed Jim Mackenzie. "Jim, we're going to sit right here," I said. "We're going to wait until Texas gets in the huddle and starts breaking before we call the defense. We're not going to get caught again. You remember what happened two years ago." Jim nodded yes. We stood and watched.

Darrell ran Hix Green in and out, and Ernie Koy in and out. Finally, Koy left and Green came back. We knew if they were going to run the ball, they'd want big, tough Ernie Koy in there. We went to our "defend" defense and rushed Kristynik before he had time for any protection or for the pattern to develop. The pass for Hix Green was short, low, and incomplete. I thought, "Lawsy mercy, if we'd lost that game on the same type situation as the '62 game, I believe I'd have shot myself."

Darrell is one of the most intensely competitive men I've ever known, but he was always as totally gracious in defeat (although he never had much practice) as he was in victory. He came to our dressing room that night to congratulate our team. He wished us well, but he warned us, "We'll be right behind you to pick up everything you drop."

Neither team lost again that year. In fact, neither team lost until we beat Texas at Fayetteville the following October, 27-24. The Razorbacks weren't scored on the rest of the 1964 season. We gave up 64 points the first five games, zero the last five, and led the nation in defense against scoring with an average yield of 5.7 points per game. We were matched with Nebraska in the Cotton Bowl. Texas drew Alabama in the first Orange Bowl games played at night.

All season, everybody figured Notre Dame a shoo-in for the national championship after we beat Texas. This was a big Irish revival year under Ara Parseghian, and there was no question that an undefeated Notre Dame team would sweep the polls. At the end, though, the Irish were knocked off by Southern Cal. The final wire service poll showed undefeated Alabama No. 1, undefeated Arkansas No.2.

In those days, the wire services did not make a final survey after the bowl games. Apparently it had never been much of an issue before. Texas beat Alabama in the Orange Bowl (Joe Namath's last college game) and we beat Nebraska in the Cotton, 10-7. Then Arkansas was the only undefeated team in major-college football, but the wire service polls had closed in November. We were national champions in the view of the Football Writers of America, which awarded us the Grantland Rice Trophy after the bowl games, and of course in our own view. We were the only undefeated team left, and we had beat Texas, which beat Alabama.

Texas had a great linebacker, Tommy Nobis, who played for an 11-0 team as a sophomore in '63 and a 10-1 team in '64. Coming up to his senior season, he had lost only once as a varsity athlete—to Arkansas in the 14-13 game. What about Arkansas, Nobis was asked during the spring of 1965. "I think about Arkansas a little bit every day," Nobis said. "We all do." That's what you call bulletin board material. We made certain our players were aware of Tommy's thoughts that fall.

We led the nation in defense in '64, and turned around with a larger, faster, and more specialized squad in 1965 which led the country in scoring. Our average was 32.4 points per game. Although we were on a 12-game winning streak when the season opened, Texas was the conference favorite. Along with Nobis, the Horns had several outstanding veterans who would prosper in the pros—Pete Lammons, Diron Talbert, John Elliott.

When we kicked off at Fayetteville in a nationally televised game on the afternoon of October 16, 1965, both teams were 4-0 for the season. Texas was rated No. 1 in the nation, Arkansas No. 3. We were prepared for anything except what happened. By the middle of the second quarter, Arkansas led by 20-0. It might just as easily have been 34-0; we had two touchdowns called back. Martine Bercher covered a bobbled punt in the end zone for one touchdown. Tommy Trantham caught a fumble in the air and ran 77 yards for another score. Brittenum passed to Crockett for a third. Penalties wiped out TD passes to Crockett and Harry Jones.

The Horns started rolling with some well-planned misdirection stuff. Darrell did a magnificent job of picking our "monster" defense apart like no one had ever done before. Their quarterback, Kristynik, would fake the option play one way and then throw back the other way. They did a lot of things we hadn't seen before, all designed to catch our monster man out of place. They were able to move the ball and score, and, by the half, they had closed the gap to 20-11. I've read that Darrell walked into the Texas dressing room at the half and wrote "21-20" on the blackboard. In essence, he was telling them, "We've got a good thing going, just stick to your knitting, stay with the game plan."

In the second half, Texas appeared to have taken control of the game. We had poor field position so we didn't want to pass, and they crowded us with an eight-man front. They went ahead of us, 21-20. David Conway's third field goal of the game made it 24-20. We didn't have a first down from the second quarter until near the end of the fourth. Our winnnig streak seemed about to end in a game in which a 20-point lead got away from us. We were sick and stunned on the sidelines.

We took over on our 20 for our last shot at it. We had to go 80 yards against the wind with time running out. Definitely not a bright prospect for a team that hadn't moved the ball in nearly three periods. "Jim Lindsey is the one who rallied our team," I told everybody after the game. "Not me. I was a babbling idiot."

Lindsey reminded the offensive unit that Texas was not double-covering Crockett. He pointed out that if they did start doubling Crockett, something else would open up. We went for the winning touchdown with nine men blocking and Crockett as the only pass receiver out. Brittenum completed six passes, and Crockett made a leaping catch of the last one and fell on the flag at the corner. Brittenum sneaked the ball across with 1:32 to play, and, according to Dan Jenkins in *Sports Illustrated,* as Brittenum scored, "a national television audience and all of Arkansas saw helmets sail into the air almost as high as Broyles jumped."

"I'd never take credit for what Crockett and Brittenum did," Lindsey told me years later. "Crockett was lunging and diving and leaping all over the field. I just put into words what was in everybody's gut."

Jim was bothered by rib injuries most of his senior year and played little in the Texas game. He went in for the last drive and started it with a seven-yard carry on first down. "If I'd been on the field all day, I might have felt the momentum shift and I might have felt that we didn't have a chance," he said. "But from where I was sitting, I didn't think we were beat."

The following week, the Razorbacks were ranked No. 1 in a national wire-service poll for the first and only time in their history. We slipped back because we didn't have the intersectional voting strength to hold first place, but we didn't worry much about it. This time, the Associated Press agreed to wait until after the bowls to issue its final ranking.

We finished 10-0, giving us perfect seasons back to back and a 22-game winning streak. Michigan State and Nebraska also finished with 10-0 records. All three of us lost in the bowls. Alabama had it both ways. The Crimson Tide took the Associated Press award in 1964 because the AP wouldn't wait for the bowls; the Tide received it again in '65 (with a 9-1-1 record) because the AP did wait.

Lindsey Nelson, who handled play-by-play on the 1965 Arkansas-Texas game for NBC-TV, called it the best college game he'd ever seen. Johnny Vaught, the Ole Miss coach, told me not long after that game, "Frank, if you ever feel down and discouraged, just pull out that film and look at it."

Darrell's team lost four of its last six for a 6-4 season after starting out with every intention of winning the national championship. Once, in a telephone conversation, I tried to tell Darrell how the adversity of our 5-5 season in '63 had helped push us on to two perfect seasons. I reminded him of how he tried to pep me up while we were losing six straight in '58, and that dismal streak turned around into three straight championships. He seemed to feel encouraged before we hung up, but a week or two later—after another loss—he called back.

"Frank, about this adversity stuff. You think maybe I'm overdoing it?"

In 1966 at Austin, Martine Bercher opened things up for us with a 59-yard punt return to the Texas 16 and we won a very tough game 12-7 for three in a row over Texas. That day, Darrell was determined to run toward our monster man every down, rather than try to block all the stunts he would see on the weakside, away from the monster. Once we realized this, we made an in-game adjustment, and we had probably our best defensive game against them. Darrell is hard-headed, like most good football coaches. He had a game plan and he was going to make it work. He stayed with his plan the entire ball game, and that's the only time I was ever surprised (pleasantly surprised, I mean) by any of his decisions in a game.

Texas and Arkansas both missed the boat in '66 and '67, the only two years in the decade that the Southwest Conference championship landed somewhere other than Fayetteville or Austin. The Razorbacks and Horns played on national TV at Little Rock in '67, although we were headed for 4-5-1 and Texas was on the way to its third straight 6-4 season. Texas beat us, 21-12. We tried an onsides kick after cutting it to 14-12, but Texas covered the ball and drove it in for a clinching touchdown.

Both teams underwent fundamental changes before we got together again at Austin in '68: Darrell switched to the wishbone offense and placed it in the hands of James Street, a fire-eating leader at quarterback. We had a sophomore quarterback, Bill Montgomery, running our version of the Florida State offense, which let us mix pro-type passing with our standard running game. The substitution rules had relaxed to the point where two-platoon football was a full reality again. It was a new age of specialization, and football offenses were opening up all over the country. "Risk-taking became promiscuous," is the way Orville Henry put it once. While everybody talked of offense, our '68 defensive unit either scored or directly set up 28 of our 49 touchdowns.

We went to Austin with a 4-0 record. Texas was tied by Houston and suffered a conference loss to Texas Tech before the wishbone exploded, so nobody had any idea what to expect. For awhile, it seemed more like a track meet or a tennis match than a football game. Texas finally won it, 39-29. Some people claim that was the only 39-29 score in the history of college football. I don't know, and I've never been inclined to try to look it up.

Arkansas and Texas tied for the conference title, and of course the Longhorns drew the Cotton Bowl bid because of their win over us. We went to the Sugar Bowl to play an undefeated (twice tied) Georgia team loaded with pro prospects (Jake Scott, Bill Stanfill). Paul "Bear" Bryant of Alabama told people that Georgia was the best team in the country at the end of the regular season. The Southwest Conference never had a prouder holiday season. Hayden Fry's SMU team outlasted Oklahoma in a wild Bluebonnet Bowl game. Texas blasted Tennessee in the Cotton. Arkansas shocked the Southeastern Conference by beating Georgia, 16-2. I still think that Georgia team may have had the most physically gifted defensive unit the Razorbacks ever played against. Our defense intercepted three Georgia passes and recovered five fumbles. Chuck Dicus, who set a Sugar Bowl record with 12 catches for 169 yards, beat Scott deep for the game's only touchdown. Bob White kicked three field goals.

In 1969, ABC-TV wanted a showpiece game for early December to properly climax the 100th season of college football. Arkansas vs. Texas at Fayetteville was the network's choice. Would the schools agree to switch the game to December 6? Everybody was for it except Barnie. "By December 6," he said, "you might be playing for the championship of Washington County." We knew we had to have AstroTurf for Razorback Stadium because we often get ice and snow at Fayetteville in December, but there was no way either school or the Conference could turn down the opportunity. When all the revisions were made, the TV football schedule that fall was worth about $1,500,000 to the SWC and its member schools.

Everything worked like a charm. When game day finally arrived,

Broyles, Royal, and Fry celebrate a great "Bowling" season for the Southwest Conference.

Texas was 9-0 and No. 1 in the nation, and Arkansas was 9-0 and No. 2 in the nation.

The switch was a break for us in more ways than one. We were more physically able to play Texas in December than we would have been in the regular October spot. Chuck Dicus hurt his shoulder against Baylor. Bill Montgomery missed the spring work because of shoulder surgery stemming from an injury in the Sugar Bowl game. Bill's passing didn't come all the way back until late in the season. We had a tough time beating TCU, 24-6, and Baylor, 21-7. Texas was just snowballing over everybody. A lot of people compared our scores to the Longhorns' scores against the same opponents, and decided we didn't have a chance in the world. That was okay with us, so long as we didn't start thinking that way.

I don't want to fall in the trap of comparing individuals and teams, but our defensive unit of 1969 was (along with the 1964 group and one or two others) a serious candidate for the best we ever had. Charley Coffey, the defensive coordinator, and Bob Ford scouted Texas for Big Shootout I, and they did a magnificent job of plotting a defense for the wishbone that looked unstoppable. Darrell has told me that he thinks the longest run the Longhorns made from the line of scrimmage (other than the famous broken play by Street) was eight yards. It was a fantastic job. We played stunts off a 6-2 that Texas hadn't seen before, and couldn't fathom. Outside linebacker Mike Boschetti and monster man Bobby Field served the same function as defensive ends. We had Bruce James, Rick Kersey, Dick Bumpas, and Roger Harnish inside. Cliff Powell and Lynn Garner were the linebackers. Terry Stewart, Jerry Moore, and Dennis Berner formed the three-deep secondary.

All during the game, we wondered just how long we could contain them with our surprise defense. According to Darrell, it was impossible for them to adjust during the game to all the things we were doing defensively.

When the helicopter carrying President Nixon and his party landed on the practice field adjacent to Razorback Stadium, Arkansas already held a 7-0 lead. Field recovered a fumble at the Texas 22 on the second play of the game. Split end John Rees made a great catch going out of bounds with a Montgomery pass at the two on third down, and Bill Burnett pushed in for the touchdown.

Texas had a history of jumping into an 8-3, with man-for-man coverage, when you hit their 35-yard line—to try to turn you around with a big loss, a bad play. To counteract this alignment, we designed a big play for Chuck Dicus. If we found them in an 8-3, we were going to change from a run to a pass at the line of scrimmage. We thought we could score with Dicus having "man" coverage to the weakside. It never worked more beautifully. The play was called back, however, because Rees, who did not pick up the audible, went down and threw a block at a defensive back. He made no contact, and even if he had his action was insignificant to the play, which was to the wide side of the field and he was on the short side. We hadn't gone over the play enough in the short time that we had in order to impress upon him that he should do nothing except trot down the field and occupy somebody. If it was a pass, it was away from him; if it was a run, it was away from him. When a player makes a mistake in a situation like that coaches can only blame themselves because they didn't go over it two or three more times. This was such a key part of our plan—to get an easy and early touchdown off the Texas 8-3. The nullified score would have given us a 14-0 lead after two possessions.

Dicus, usually coming out of the slot, caught nine passes for 146 yards. Montgomery, scrambling like a demon under constant pressure from a great defense, produced our second touchdown in two great plays. After a fumble recovery in the third quarter gave us the ball on our 47, Bill scrambled for 18 yards and then drilled a 29-yard touchdown pass to Dicus.

Going into the fourth quarter, Arkansas held a 14-0 lead and Texas hadn't been able to get anything going. The times Street had tried to throw deep to his fine receiver, Cotton Speyrer, Stewart and Berner made interceptions. As the fourth quarter started, Texas faced third-and-long on our 42. Street wasn't much of a passer but he was a great scrambler and leader. We knew if we got Texas into a situation where he had to pass, we were going to rush Street hard. The occasion presented itself here. Texas "broke" the wishbone and went into a spread, and Cliff Powell, our defensive signal-caller changed the defense to a rush. Street couldn't find his intended receiver in time and took off running. When he passed the line of scrimmage there were very few people left to get him. We'd rushed seven men, and one of the other four slipped on the wet AstroTurf. Street went 42 yards to score. Darrell had already determined he was going for two points the first time he scored, and Street made it on a counter-option carry.

We came back with a beautiful drive. A penalty wiped out a 20-yard pass to Dicus, so Montgomery came back with the same play and completed it again. This drive led to a national championship decision that went wrong. If it goes right, boy, you win everything. I've pondered over it for years, as I'm sure many of our fans have. I guess the single biggest decision of my career was made as we neared the goal line on that fourth-quarter drive. ·

Texas had a habit of "pounding" your receivers, especially as you neared their goal line. One of the Longhorns' defenders was detected holding up Dicus, and Texas drew a pass interference penalty that put us on their eight. It was always tough to try to punch the ball in against Texas from as far out as the eight, so we came back with another pass. They interfered with Dicus again—just as badly as on the penalty call, we thought, but it wasn't called twice in a row. We tried a running play that went nowhere, so we had third-and-eight on the right hash-mark.

A field goal looked just as important as a touchdown at that time. With a field goal, we'd have had 17 points and a nine-point lead against a team we had contained all day. We had a staff meeting and considered all the options. If we ran and set up the ball in the middle of the goal posts, we'd have a sophomore, Bill McClard, kicking. Also, we had to consider that Rodney Brand, our All-American center, would be snapping on field goals, and we'd had a couple of bad snaps during the year. Rodney, a fine blocker, was the best long-snapper we had at the time, but he was just adequate in that category. We talked about the gambles we'd be taking on a field goal. Then our coaches up in the press box brought out the point that on the goal line, Texas defensive back Danny Lester lined up way inside. They figured Dicus could beat him for an easy touchdown. Montgomery could roll that way and throw the ball. If Dicus was covered, Montgomery could throw it out of bounds and we could go on and kick the field goal on fourth down from the angle.

I decided in favor of going for the touchdown pass and, as I recall, it worked just as we planned—up to a point. Dicus broke out and he was wide open. As Montgomery told me later, he "aimed" the football. Dicus was so wide open, Bill wanted to be careful and he under-threw it just a little bit. That gave Lester, who lined up inside and was intially defeated on the play, a chance to break in front of Dicus and intercept. Bill had not thrown for an interception in about 80 passes covering five or six ball games. If he had just floated the ball in there, or led Dicus properly, it would have been a sure touchdown, and a clinching touchdown. Texas drove out to midfield and fumbled. On the Longhorns' next possession, Darrell faced fourth-and-three at the Texas 43. That's when he went for a bomb to the tight end, Randy Peschel.

"Sometimes," Darrell said in the dressing room later that day, "you just have to suck it up and pick a number." Darrell told me later that they went for the all-or-nothing pass because they knew they couldn't score from 50 yards out with their regular offense. They didn't have time to grind it out on an afternoon when they hadn't made more than eight or nine yards with a designed running play. Making a first down at midfield at that late stage wouldn't help him,

Darrell figured, so he went for broke—a long pass on fourth down with only one receiver out. Street made a good fake that drew up our secondary a little, and Peschel got loose on a route down the sideline. Moore and Berner jumped, and the ball appeared to go right between them. Neither could quite get a hand on it. Peschel caught it for a 44-yard advance to our 11. Ted Koy broke to the two, and Jim Bertelsen followed big Steve Wooster through for the touchdown on an inside belly move. The Texas place-kicker with the captivating name of Happy Feller kicked the Longhorns ahead, 15-14.

We came back and reached the Texas 39 and one more pass completion would have put us in McClard's range. Montgomery threw the ball a little bit "up for grabs" and Tom Campbell of Texas was able to pull it away from Rees for an interception.

On a day when we held the nation's full attention, Texas and Arkansas played one of the classic games in football history. Our team was well prepared by our coaches, they gave a heroic effort, and we outplayed them most of the game. Despite all the praise that came our way, however, Texas won and went on to the Cotton Bowl against Notre Dame, which was ending its long, self-imposed bowl ban.

It had been worked out in advance that the loser of the Arkansas-Texas game would go to the Sugar Bowl against Ole Miss. We had a lot of trouble settling down in the Sugar Bowl game, but when we did, we made 537 yards. Bruce Maxwell ran through the Rebels all day. Dicus caught six passes for 171 yards. Montgomery piled up 338 yards of total offense. But after all this we still lost 27-22. We were slow to adjust to all the things Archie Manning could do, and were behind 24-6 before we really got moving. McClard had the only really bad day of his kicking career. Texas, then undefeated in 20 straight games, clinched the national championship in an exciting victory over Notre Dame.

Everything had worked so well that ABC asked for a Big Shootout II in December of 1970. We had some rebuilding to do, particularly on defense. We also were opening the '70 season in a TV game against Stanford University and Jim Plunkett. We fell behind Stanford, 27-0, and ended up losing 34-28 when they stopped us on fourth down inside the five at the finish. That was our third straight heartbreaker on national television. We won our next nine, most of them impressively. Bill Burnett was hurt in the Texas A&M game, and after that we seemed to have a rash of injuries, so we were patching rather desperately as we approached Big Shootout II.

For a solid year, the Texas players had heard how lucky they were to have escaped Fayetteville with a one-point win. To me, this was the greatest of all the Texas teams—the 1970 crowd with Eddie Phillips running the wishbone, and of course Wooster and Bertelsen and all of them. Barry Switzer, then an assistant to Chuck Fairbanks at Oklahoma, gave me a warning in midseason. Oklahoma had tried to use our 1969 defense against Texas. "You had success with it as a change-of-pace surprise," Barry said. "They've worked all spring and fall on it. Let me tell you, Coach, don't line up in that defense. They're gonna eat you alive, like they did us."

Coffey and I had a big argument. He wanted to play what we'd played the year before. I tried to convince him that Texas was ready for it, and we debated, and finally I had to order him to put in another defense—the first time I ever did that with a defensive coordinator. I told him to put in a "50" defense and get it ready for the Texas game, and we didn't play it very well. Coffey had no confidence in it, and he may have been right. I don't think that cost us the ball game because Texas was great and really prepared, and they might have moved the ball against any defense that day. We kept it competitive into the third quarter, but they wound up handing us the worst defeat an Arkansas team suffered in my time, 42-7. As you may recall, the game turned when we failed to punch in from the one for a 14-14 tie; instead Texas drove 99 yards for a 21-7 lead. Coffey left for a head-coaching job at Virginia Tech after the game.

Although we finished with a 9-2 record, we were shut out of the bowl picture. An "either-or" arrangement was struck with the Sugar Bowl the previous year, but no bowl was willing to wait for the loser of the Arkansas-Texas game in '70. As things turned out, it was just as well.

That was the only time in 19 years that a team scored 40 or more points against our Razorbacks' defense. Here's as illustration of what a constant factor our defense had been through the 1960s: If we had scored at least two touchdowns in every game we played, we'd have won 15 more games in our first 10 seasons. As it was, we only lost 29 over that period.

Generally, we did not have the muscle to play Texas after they went to the wishbone. In the hands of a great physical squad like

Texas (or, later, Oklahoma and Alabama) the wishbone is an awesome offense because it tends to magnify physical superiority. As time went along, most coaches (including me) came to prefer the veer as an option offense most readily adaptable to most situations. If you have an instinctive triple-option quarterback and plenty of healthy running backs, the wishbone isn't obsolete. Of course, if you have the proper personnel you can win with anything—players are always going to be more important than formations. But the defenses caught up with average wishbone teams and average wishbone quarterbacks, just as defenses caught up with the split-T and everything else in the past.

With the wishbone, Texas made six straight trips to the Cotton Bowl. In yet another nationally televised match-up, we beat them in the rain at Little Rock in 1971, 31-7, on Joe Ferguson's finest day as a Razorback. That was the only Southwest Conference game Darrell lost from early in 1968 until 1974.

In a night TV game that started in a driving rain in Austin in '72, we asserted some ball control with our own wishbone, and reached the half with a 9-7 lead—thanks to three field goals by Mike Kirkland. A high snap on a punt undid us in the second half and Texas came on to win, 35-15. We didn't have the experience, stability, and strength to cope with them in 1973 (34-6) and '74 (38-7). By 1975, we'd put together a squad of championship caliber, but we lost to Texas at Fayetteville, 24-18, on a day when both teams erred repeatedly. "Both of us tried to join the national government in the giveaway program," Darrell said after the game.

That year, ABC-TV matched us with Texas A&M in December, and the network got its money's worth. Texas A&M came in with a 10-0 record and a tremendous defensive unit. The Aggies were thinking about a national championship; we were thinking about a seldom-used Southwest Conference policy. If three teams finished in a first-place tie, and no one held wins over both the others, the Cotton Bowl bid went to the school that had been absent from the Cotton Bowl the longest. In this case, that was us. The Aggies had to beat Texas. They did by 20-10. We had to beat the Aggies. We did by 31-6 in a great, great shocker.

The network selected Texas-Arkansas as the December game for 1976, but this time Darrell and I were both headed for 5-5-1 records. We were chatting on the telephone in midseason, and Darrell

Frank and Darrell meet at midfield as the Razorbacks and the Longhorns warm up for the last time under the two.

griped about various aspects of recruiting. "I'm going to leave all that with you," I said. "I'll tell you something if you'll keep it under your hat. I'm quitting. This is my last year."

Darrell was quiet for a few seconds. Then he said, "All right, I'll tell you something if you'll keep it quiet. I'm quitting, too. This is my last year. We'll go out together."

Nothing was official until after the game, but the word was already out on our decisions, and that sort of "saved" the game from television's standpoint, although that was just a happy coincidence. The only suspense during Texas' 29-12 victory involved whether or not the Razorbacks' Ben Cowins would make enough yardage to lead the conference in rushing (he did) and otherwise it was Auld Lang Syne all the way. We met at midfield for the last time with a crowd of reporters and cameramen around us. Later, one of the writers asked Darrell: "Didn't I hear one of your say, 'I love you'?"

"Well, you might have," Darrell said. "We do, anyway."

Several times since that night at Austin, I've jokingly told Darrell if I'd known he was getting out, I might have stayed on longer. At least, I think I was joking.

16
THE WILL OF THE PEOPLE

According to the record book, the Razorbacks' 22-game winning streak started with a 27-20 victory over Texas Tech on November 23, 1963. It actually had its beginnings one week earlier, at the low point of a miserable season.

We had lost to SMU by 14-7, putting us at 4-5 in a year in which we'd been picked to win the conference championship. We were terrible that day in Dallas. On the way home, I was sitting on the plane as low as I could be when I looked up and saw six or seven of the seniors-to-be coming toward me: Jerry Lamb, Ronnie Caveness, Fred Marshall. . . . I can't be sure now which six or seven it was, because before the plane ride was over all the people who were going to be seniors the following years were caught up in it. So was the rest of the squad.

"Coach, we're so disappointed in ourselves that we just don't know anything to tell you except that you're gonna see a new football team. Monday we want to go out and scrimmage. We want to win this last game, and next year we're going to be a great football team."

That was music to my ears, but they said a lot more. They went on about how they had let themselves down, how they thought they were going to win by just walking out on the field, and they hadn't worked like they should. As sophomores in '62 they'd been part of a winning team (9-1), and everything had seemed so easy and automatic. It was a very serious, very moving, very honest discussion.

Ordinarily we had little contact work during the season and never on Monday, but we went out the next week and put on the pads Monday, Tuesday, and Wednesday and got after it like we were back in two-a-days. We beat Texas Tech on the weekend that the country was shocked and grieved by the assassination of President Kennedy, and we did not lose until Louisiana State upset us in the Cotton Bowl on January 1, 1966. We came out of that 5-5 season in '63 with a 22-game winning streak.

After the job Billy Gray did while substituting for the injured Billy Moore in the Sugar Bowl the previous January, we figured Gray would be our quarterback in '63. Gray was so quick, such a talented all-round athlete, we thought he could be a great quarterback. While we were getting ready to play in the fall of '63, Billy told us he didn't want to be a quarterback. He'd rather play full-time on defense. We went with him against Oklahoma State and won 21-0, and then lost to Missouri 7-6 (in a one-shot intersectional game that I'm sure gives some long-memoried Missouri fans a great deal of satisfaction).

Then we were coming up to the TCU game, the conference opener where we'd traditionally put it all together each year. Doug Dickey, the offensive coach, said, "Frank, if we're going to be any good this year, Freddy Marshall has got to be the quarterback." Fred, from Memphis, had been redshirted one year and had served as the third-string quarterback behind Moore and Gray in '62. This was his fourth year around. "Fine," I said. "We'll go with him." Marshall started against TCU and we won 18-3. However, we had to turn to Gray again late in the game. Marshall threw four passes and three of them should have been intercepted. Lamb saved one with a fantastic catch that he just absolutely took away from a TCU defender. We studied the film and said to ourselves, "Freddy's not ready." Then we went from quarterback to quarterback: Brittenum, Gray, Marshall. Finally, in the SMU game, we found Marshall had to be the quarterback. We were miserable that day, as I've said, but Fred played well until he was hurt. He started against Tech in the last game, and came back his fifth year and led us to an 11-0 season and the national championship. I look back and wish we'd stuck with Fred in '63. Instead of 5-5, we might have won eight or nine games. However, when I think how much that disappointing season meant in setting the foundations for '64 and '65, I find no reason to quibble about anything. Sometimes you have to get worse before you can get better.

It's hard to explain the chemistry of certain situations. We had good athletes and, collectively, they made up their minds they were going to win. Nothing would stop them. Easy to say, but hard to define, and impossible to create unless the feeling just springs naturally from your players.

The substitution rules were relaxed a little more in 1964, and we made a staff decision in the spring that we would prepare players only one way in spring practice, and hope that we could use time-outs and incomplete passes to switch our units around without us getting hurt. College football was definitely on a trend back toward two-platoon football, and we all rejoiced. The specialized game is so much better for players, coaches, and fans. One-platoon football leads to "two yards and cloud of dust" eras, as was proved in the 1950s. Anyway, we started out in '64 with the players' complete dedication, with our quarterback in mind, with a favorable rule change, and a new offense that suited us perfectly.

At Southern Cal in '62, John McKay won a national championship with a revamped "I" formation. The "I" had been sort of a gimmick offense when it first appeared, but McKay put two wide receivers on it. McKay wanted our Arkansas monster defense, and we made an informal swap: give us the "I" and we'll give you the monster. I always had great respect for J. T. King of Texas Tech as an offensive thinker, and I had admired his modifications of McKay's offense. We adapted it into the wide slot-I and won the first 21 times we lined up in it.

I wanted something where we could use the old "fly" we'd used at Georgia Tech and fake off tackle and throw in the flat to the wingback. As I got into the "I" formation, I realized that if we could put a wingback out there, who could serve the purpose of a tight end on occasion, and be a threat going back the other way, and a great pass receiver, everything would open up. Then we could run off-tackle, and when the off-tackle play was stopped, we had a two-man pass pattern: the end deep and the halfback in the flat.

I remember that at a coaches' convention I told Murray Warmath and Woody Hayes what we planned to do, and they kind of giggled about it. Woody ran that formation as long as he coached. Nebraska and Michigan are still doing basically the same things we did with the "I" formation in '64.

We had the perfect wingback for it in Jim Lindsey, the perfect tailback in Bobby Burnett, the perfect fullback in Bobby Nix (who blocked and blocked and blocked), and the perfect quarterback in Marshall (and then Brittenum). "If Alworth could have played that position (wingback in the wide-slot I), he'd have averaged nine yards a carry and no telling what he would have accumulated as a receiver," Jim Lindsey said. "He would have been unbelievable. It allowed me to develop the flexibility to play in the pros as somewhat of a running back and a reserve receiver. It was suited to every skill I had."

One snowy day in the winter of 1979, I visited Lindsey's office in Fayetteville to talk about the winning streak. The same drive and perceptiveness that made Jim such a valuable football player for the Razorbacks and the Minnesota Vikings predictably carried over into his post-football career as a successful real estate developer. I knew I could count on him to remember everything.

"You players ran us coaches out of the dressing room at Texas Tech," I said, referring to the game that sealed our perfect season in '64.

Jim laughed, "Yes, we did," he said.

"What did you talk about?"

"Caveness and Lamb were on opposite sides of the dressing room. Lamb had dropped a pass in the first half, wide open. He started crying in the dressing room. 'Cuz', he said to Caveness, 'we've been playing ball together for 10 years; this is our last game.' Then Caveness started crying. Pretty soon everybody was crying. That wasn't any great trick for me; I was always really kinda tearful when we really got into something. But we had a couple of guys who were kinda cold and cynical about all that rah-rah stuff, and I looked at them and they were wiping tears just like everybody else. It was 0-0 at the half, and Texas Tech didn't have any more chance of winning that game after we left that dressing room . . . than if they'd re-cruited the backfield of the Chicago Bears. It was over right then. The emotional structure of that situation could never be equaled. Lamb took a pass away from a Texas Tech man in the end zone in the second half.

"If you can get enough people dreaming ways that you can win, and not accept the other side, you've got it. You can have all sorts of convictions about winning games or changing the country or whatever, but if you don't have an equal commitment, you're gonna end up in confusion. We had conviction and commitment in equal parts. Each Thursday at the squad meeting, the upperclassmen would get up and say their little statement for the week, and Jerry Jones always got up last and always said the same thing. 'Men, it ain't but about 10 steps from the penthouse to the outhouse. Don't ever forget that.'"

"How did that story go about Jones in the Baylor game of '64?" I asked.

"We had driven the ball practically the length of the field," Lindsey said. "About a 20-play drive, seemed like. I ran a throwback pattern and was wide open; I can still see it right now. Freddy Marshall threw the ball back inside for Lamb, and Bobby Maples intercepted at the end zone and took off down the sideline and all of us took off after him. Down around our 28 or 30, Glen Ray Hines hit him from behind, and he fumbled and Jones recovered the ball.

"Well, it was hot that night. Our offense had been on the field a long time driving, then we had to chase down the pass interception, then we had the ball back with all that distance to cover, and here was the referee cranking it right up again. And in the huddle, Jones was really sucking air. We were all exhausted, gasping, and you know how Wilson Matthews and some of the other coaches were always talking about 'character.' As we broke the huddle, I can still hear Jones: 'Boys, if we can take this blankety-blank thing in from here, we've got some character.' We made about three first downs before we had to punt.

"The guys who really won championships for us in that day and time were probably completely different than the top physical athlete of today. Guys like Bobby Roper, Charlie Daniel. Nobody can really know just how intense Roper played and how much he cared about winning. How much he felt it was good and meaningful to win, the right side of winning. It wasn't for himself. Like he blocked those two kicks in the Texas Tech game. Down to the last game, and we've got to have it, and I don't think he'd ever blocked a field goal before."

This was the unit that led the nation in defense against scoring in 1964 and shut out our last five opponents: LE—Jim Finch, 204. LT—Loyd Phillips, 220. LLB—Ronnie Mac Smith, 190. MG—Jimmy Johnson, 200. RLB—Ronnie Caveness, 212. RT—Jim Williams, 204. RE—Bobby Roper, 193. MM—Charles Daniel, 185, and LH—Billy Gray, 170 (also a back-up at quarterback). RH—Ken Hatfield, 170. S—Harry Jones, 195.

And this was the offensive unit that got better and better after an unpromising two or three games until it reached the point where it executed with nearly error-free efficiency: WE—Bobby Crockett, 189. WT—Glen Ray Hines, 232. WG—Jerry Welch, 210. C—Randy Stewart, 204. SG—Jerry Jones, 200. SE—Jerry Lamb, 185. QB—Fred Marshall, 180. TB—Jack Brasuell, 175, and Bobby Burnett,190. WB—Jim Lindsey, 198. FB—Bobby Nix, 193. Nix punted, and Tom McKnelly place-kicked.

We had the best spring practice in 1964 that I saw in all my time in coaching. From the motivational standpoint, the coaches didn't have to say a word. All spring it was as if we were getting ready to play Texas every day. Caveness held the key to the defense, and I came down hard on him at a squad meeting on the back of the freshmen practice field at the start of the spring. I reminded him, with the whole squad listening, that he'd had a terrific sophomore year in '62, and that he couldn't have been satisfied with his performance as a junior. I told him he was either going to stay and help us be a great football team, or he was going to leave and help us. I knew the answer in advance, but this was sort of a final air-clearing session to emphasize that the coaching staff was as serious as the players said they were. Ronnie made All-American—great linebacker, great leader. That squad had so many great leaders. There was closeness that I never found in any other football team, and to this day I believe they remain our most closely knit group of former athletes.

Marshall hurt his shoulder in a practice a few days before the Oklahoma State opener. He started, but he couldn't pass and we had to go back to Billy Gray to take us to a 14-10 victory that didn't have much of a national championship look about it. In fact, we were picked way down in the Southwest Conference that year. The experts were badly burned when they made us favorites the year before.

In both '64 and '65, we had to beat two of the best Tulsa teams of recent times (Howard Twilley, Jerry Rhome, etc.). In '64, with Marshall out, we fell behind Tulsa 14-0 and were badly outdone in the statistics. Caveness turned it around for us with a pass interception for a touchdown and fumble recovery. We just barely survived with a 31-22 win.

The real Fred Marshall took over in the TCU game and everything fit into place, 29-6. Marshall accounted for more than 200 yards passing and running in the 17-6 win over Baylor.

"What do you remember about the Texas game?" I asked Lindsey.

"A miracle," he said. "I looked at the film again just a few years ago, and I don't see how we won. When I think about the Texas game, I always remember what Groundy (trainer Bill Ferrell) said. The night before we saw the movie *Fail-Safe*. As we were getting taped, some of us were talking about the possibility of the world blowing up, and I said, 'What did you think about *Fail-Safe,* Groundy? You think there's anything to that?' He replied, 'Lindsey, I don't know about *Fail-Safe,* but I do know some boys that's gonna get their—beat if they don't start thinking about Texas!'

"Groundy liked to repeat an old Bowden Wyatt story, and he thought it especially applied to that Texas game. When Arkansas beat Ole Miss 6-0 (in 1954), Bowden ran out all the assistant coaches when he talked to the squad. Groundy stayed in, because he was working on somebody. Bowden said, 'Men, we've watched 'em warm up; they've got a bunch of gazelles out there. If you've studied the films, you know they're better than us. The man across from you is better than you. You can look at the program and tell they're bigger than us. If you even glanced on their end of the field while we were warming up, you know they're faster than us. They're bigger and faster and better, but somehow under God we're gonna beat those blankety-blanks!' Groundy told a bunch of us that story. When we beat Texas down there (14-13), Lamb was just ecstatic. He usually didn't say much, but that night, he just kept repeating that last Bowden phrase to everybody.

"After that, it was just the will of the people, you might say. There was almost nobody on the team concerned with his personal performance, as judged by the people who saw them, but they were all desperately concerned about whether we could pull this deal off (go undefeated). I don't believe there's ever been a team that could report in the condition we were in that fall. You just can't come back weighing 255 or '60 pounds and be equal to what Glen Ray Hines was at 232 when he could weigh 270 as easy as they can today. And Mike Bender at 218, Dick Cunningham around 216. Some of these guys could run a 440 relay and compete against a good high school track team. Jim Williams (defensive tackle) ran a 10.2 or 10.3 in the 100 over at Forrest City all the time in high school. I know things have changed and it's a completely different brand of football, but, as far as physical stamina, teams today could not come back in as good a condition as we were in that year. There's no way."

After Texas, we settled on 17-0 as a favorite score. We beat Wichita 17-0, Texas A&M 17-0, Rice 21-0, SMU 44-0, and Texas Tech 17-0. Five straight shutouts. The 1964 Razorbacks' defense put together 21 consecutive scoreless quarters before Nebraska scored and took a 7-3 lead in the second quarter of the Cotton Bowl game. McKnelly had given us the lead with a 31-yard field goal, set up by Marshall's passes to Lamb and Lindsey. Jimmy Johnson led a great defensive stand for us after the Cornhuskers' big play man, Harry Wilson, broke a 45-yard run to our 35 in the fourth quarter. We took over on our 20 after they punted, and put on an 80-yard drive worth the national championship.

Bill Pace, who called our offense, spotted a flaw in the Nebraska defense. When the Cornhuskers rotated their secondary, one of their ends failed to compensate for a seam that opened so we sent Burnett out from tailback for a throwback pass, and then Marshall made maybe the toughest 11-yard scrambling run I ever saw from a quarterback. Pure guts. Then Lindsey was knocked down going for a pass that Marshall had to throw too quickly. Jim never really saw the ball. "I heard a little blur," he said. He got his hands up for a nearly impossible over-the-shoulder catch. A throwback pass to Lindsey, worth 27 yards, put us on the five, and Burnett took it in.

The seniors we lost included some great players (Caveness, Lamb, Ken Hatfield, Marshall), some with only moderate ability, and some who weren't even regulars. But we worried most of all that their departure might have taken from us an attitude, a winning state of mind. Looking back from this distance, it seems natural that we followed 10-0 with 10-0, but I assure you we went through at least the normal amount of patching and shuffling and worrying in the spring and summer of 1965.

In '64, we played two outstanding sophomores, defensive tackle Loyd Phillips, one of our all-timers among linemen, and safety Harry Jones. We wanted the threat of Jones' ability added to the offense in '65. First we tried him at quarterback, then shifted him to wingback. Jim Lindsey couldn't play early because of rib injuries, and Harry broke in sensationally. Jon Brittenum, redshirted in '64 after playing his sophomore year, came back mature and confident at quarterback. Bobby Burnett, who'd alternated with Jackie Brasuell at tailback in '64 (and came on great toward the end) followed up with one of the most fantastic seasons I've ever seen a running back have. A good I-back, as you know, ran 25-30 times a game and usually inside. Bobby carried 232 times (for nearly 950 yards) and did not lose a fumble. We'd lost only six fumbles in '64, but we opened up and grew so careless in '65 that we lost seven that year. We just didn't fumble.

The 1964 Razorbacks won as underdogs, crushing everybody with defense. The 1965 Razorbacks won as week-to-week favorites, crushing everybody with offense. We had another scare from Tulsa, 20-12. We had the 27-24 thriller with Texas. Otherwise, we dominated our schedule in '65: Oklahoma State 28-14; TCU 28-0; Baylor 38-7; North Texas State 55-20; Texas A&M 31-0; SMU 24-3; and Texas Tech 42-24. Tech was a very good offensive team in Donny Anderson's senior year.

The '64 Razorbacks were feverish. The '65 Razorbacks were cool and methodical. One team did the things necessary to win as underdogs; the other kept itself prepared to win as favorites. Offensively, we lined up this way in '65: WE—Richard Trail, 202. WT—Glen Ray Hines, 232. WG—Melvin Gibbs, 212. C—Randy Stewart, 205. SG—Mike Bender, 215. ST—Dick Cunningham, 215. SE—Bobby Crockett, 195. QB—Jon Brittenum. TB—Bobby Burnett. FB—Bobby Nix. WB—Jim Lindsey, 200, or Harry Jones, 193. Bob White did the place-kicking, Nix the punting. Defensively: LE—Lee Johnson, 190. LT—Loyd Phillips, 220. LLB—Joe Black, 205. MG—Guy Jones, 180. RLB—Buddy Sims, 215. RT—Jim Williams, 204. RE—Bobby Roper, 195. MM—Steve Hoehn, 200. LH—Martine Bercher, 165. RH—Tommy Trantham, 190. S—Jack Brasuell, 175.

Phillips and Hines were consensus All-Americans, and Crockett made at least one All-American team. We had 10 all-conference players in '65.

We should have been national champions again. "If there's a better team than the Razorbacks," a Houston writer remarked during the season, "then it's up in the pros somewhere." The Cotton Bowl matched us against an LSU team better than its 7-3 record. The Tigers had their injuries all through the season, particularly at quarterback; we had ours in the weeks leading up to the bowl and, of course, in the game itself when we lost Brittenum. All the psychological things that help create so many bowl upsets were in LSU's favor, but I believe we would have won, regardless, if Brittenum hadn't been hurt. We could move the ball on them, but we had trouble getting it and keeping it.

We drove 87 yards to score right off the bat on a pass to Crockett. LSU had pro-type offensive linemen and used ball control with a tough little tailback named Joe Labruzzo. With the score tied 7-7, Brittenum dislocated his shoulder leading a sweep for Harry Jones.

Frank and Hayden Fry at the Arkansas-SMU meeting in 1965.

Jon came back and played, but at nowhere near his regular effec-
tiveness. Joe Black, the linebacker who called our defensive signals,
couldn't play at all that day. LSU ended our 22-game winning streak
with a 14-7 upset that cost us a national championship.

I take some of the blame. I should have been like a wild man for
that ball game, knowing the situation—knowing how good LSU really was, and knowing how much the game meant. Jim MacKenzie
was trying to get a head coaching job, and he visited three different
schools during the bowl practice period. I wasn't as tough and demanding as I should have been. I didn't sound enough warnings,
didn't guard against enough distractions. But I still believe we would
have won if Brittenum hadn't been hurt.

"I can't speak for before and after the times we played," Lindsey
said. "All I can really relate to is that period of time. But I think, at
that time, there was such a terrific positive feeling and atmosphere.

Like it was a great honor to be one of the soldiers or crusaders or chosen few who represented Arkansas, as we broke out of the time when we hadn't been quite so good, into this history of turning the thing around. I think coaches today may almost be working at a handicap as far as the emotional response from players now.

"When Jimmy Johnson was on the coaching staff here, I asked him, 'Johnson, just how much better are these guys than we were?' He said, 'Why, the guy playing nose guard now weighs 245 or something like that, and I tried to play at 200. We had Loyd over there at 220 and Williams at about 205.' He kept on like that, and finally he said, 'You know something, Lindsey? In spite of everything, we'd find some way to beat their —.'

"And I'll guarantee you, no matter what they say about different eras or what they say about greater athletes, if you'd ask one of those guys from '64 what he thought, and if he answered from the deepest part of his being, he'd say we'd beat 'em. Now I know he would be rational enough to recognize the players might be better, and all the arguments won't mean anything. They didn't mean anything when we were playing. We weren't supposed to win then, either."

Well, I wouldn't touch that "era" argument with a 10-foot pole. Everybody understands that football players grow bigger and faster all the time, but the essential elements that go into winning remain the same, always. Those Razorbacks beat everybody we put in front of them for 22 straight games. I'm not surprised they still think they could handle anybody. In fact, I'd be shocked if they felt any other way.

17
BARBARA

He used to call promptly at six o'clock in the morning, two or three times a football season. He lived in Florida, he was a Razorback fan, and sometimes he wasn't completely sober when the sun was coming up. We never met him, but he and Barbara became fairly good friends.

"Do you know what time it is?" Barbara would ask him.

"Sure," he said. "Seven o'clock."

"Not in Arkansas," Barbara said. "It's six o'clock, and we were asleep. Could you call us back a little later?"

Barbara always answered the phone, day or night. They were always nice to Barbara, these people who called at strange hours, and soon she'd cup her hand over the phone and say. "Here, Frank, talk to him." Sometimes they weren't so nice to me.

We were lucky, though. We always had a listed phone number and in 19 seasons as Arkansas head coach, we didn't get more than 20 "crank" calls. Our friend in Florida, and two or three others like him in other parts of the country, were not cranks: They were fans who had trouble keeping track of time zones.

I never saw a crank letter, but that doesn't mean there weren't some. Barbara screened the mail at the house and threw away the abusive stuff, and my secretary, Dorothy Cain, did the same thing at the office. Sometimes I've received letters from people apologizing for their remarks in a previous letter. I didn't even know what they were talking about.

I was sensitive, and criticism bothered me, no matter how unfair or irresponsible or unfounded it might be. I'm not saying I didn't

"My mother wouldn't let me drink anything but lemonade and buttermilk when I was growing up. Barbara finally corrupted me; she introduced me to iced tea."

deserve to be criticized, but I saw no point in brooding over an abusive letter when I had so many other things to think about. I couldn't shut things like that out of my mind like some people apparently can, so I made the decision very early that I simply wouldn't look at crank mail.

You could never tell if we'd won or lost when you saw Barbara after a football game. She was always smiling, always calm, always the same. "It's only a game, Frank," she would say, when I'd start complaining about something that went wrong. She knew better than that. She was completely involved and always completely aware of what was going on in our football program, but she was able to treat it with a calm, sensible perspective. She had a lot more confidence in our athletes than I did most of the time.

We never kept a gun in the house. I'm afraid if we had, Barbara would have shot me somewhere along the way. I ran unexpected guests in on her as a matter of course, but she always expected the unexpected, and was always equal to the occasion. If it is true that not everybody can coach, then it is equally true that not everybody can be a coach's wife.

Our children adopted Barbara's attitude toward the Razorbacks. They were involved, but they were able to keep everything in balance. Hank and Betsy were the only two you might call really vocal fans. When our 1975 team met Georgia in the Cotton Bowl, we had a lot of trouble in the first half. Betsy fumed and worried and finally asked her mother, "Is it possible for me to get a message down on the field to Daddy?"

"What is it?" Barbara said.

Betsy wanted to tell me: "Daddy: Pass! Pass! Pass! Pass!"

I asked Barbara to put together some of her memories and impressions for this book, and here is the way it was from her viewpoint:

> *Frank's whole career involved traveling, so to get in the car and travel with the children was not his idea of a vacation. We seldom went anywhere out of town as a group. The few attempts that we made almost resulted in a minor disaster of one kind or another. Once we were going to take all six children for two or three days' vacation to Little Rock. We were going fishing with Alan Berry and Brick Lile. We loaded up a station wagon and headed out the back trail down Highway 23. We had just passed Elkins, which is only 10 miles or so down the road, when we had a flat tire. "Oh, well," Frank said, "this won't take long. Let's all get out and put the spare on. We'll be on our way in a few minutes."*
>
> *"Oh, no, we won't," said Jack, who was 16 then.*
>
> *"Come on," Frank said to Jack and Hank. "Let's go. We'll all work together and it won't be any problem."*
>
> *"Oh, yes, it will," Jack said. "I had a flat last night and I forgot to get the spare fixed."*
>
> *Frank got out and thumbed a ride into Elkins. A couple in a pick-up truck gave him a ride in the back. He called the office and Mervin Johnson answered. I wonder if any other assistant coach ever received instructions like this. "Mervin," Frank said, "go to my house, jack up the car there, take the back wheels off, and bring them out here to me at Elkins. I've got to have some wheels." So Mervin and Barry Switzer, who was on the staff, went to our house and took the back wheels off a car that had interchangeable tires with our*

station wagon. We made the switch, and they took our flat tire and our flat spare with them, so they'd be fixed when we got back to Fayetteville.

Another time, we started out to Little Rock with the four youngest kids. Tommy, who was about five or six then, got sick to his stomach as we were leaving town. By the time we reached Booneville, Tommy was feeling better so we stopped for some cold drinks. Dan, who was about seven then, was sick all the rest of the way to Little Rock. We were running late by then—we'd stopped at a drug store, and stopped to try to clean up the car a couple of times— and we had a station wagon full of soiled pillows and blankets, and the like. We got to Little Rock, and Frank drove straight to the Country Club. He climbed out and said, "It's time for my golf date right now." He left me in the car to drive on to the motel where we planned to stay. If I'd had a gun, that's when I would have come closest to shooting Frank, right there in the parking lot of the Little Rock Country Club.

One summer, Frank had two coaching clinic lectures on the West Coast. Instead of him flying out there, he planned to use his expense money to drive out with our entire family. We were going to Disneyland and everywhere. At this time, the twins were about three years old, and they'd sing every time they got in the car. Two songs, and two songs only. One had no lyrics except "Woe-woe, woe-woe" over and over in the ultimate monotone. They usually broke out in that one when we left home heading down Mission. If we went over North Street and they saw some ducks in the water, they sang "ducks in the water" over and over. The boys got to thinking about being in the car all those days with the girls' singing, and California lost a lot of its appeal. The more we talked, the less they wanted to go. Finally, they told Frank if he'd buy them a trampoline, they'd stay at home and be perfectly happy. Frank said, "You get a trampoline tomorrow!" So that was the end of that trip.

The children never thought of Frank as anything but Daddy as they were growing up. Somewhere along the line, when they were in about the sixth grade, they would suddenly realize—and it's a very difficult thing to happen to you—that some people were their friends because of their father and not because they liked them. This was a problem they had to cope with, every one of them. I had been warned. Alice Dodd told me before we left Atlanta that this kind of

Linda and Betsy around 14.

thing was the biggest problem her children had to face: recognizing there would be people who would like them because it opened the way for doing things they couldn't do otherwise–going to the stadium and so forth.

And there's also the reverse of this, the discovery that some people will be hostile toward them because of their father and not because of them. We found this particularly true in the school system. I think every one of our children–I know all our boys did, and Betsy; I'm not sure it ever happened to Linda–ran into this somewhere along the line. A teacher would say, "You can't get away with that just because you're the coach's son (or daughter)." I wonder how many times a teacher has said to a child, "You can't get away with that just because your father is the plumber!"

Our lives are an open book. Everybody knows what we're doing all the time. There are very few professions where the newspaper devotes a page a day, just about, to what you're doing–not only Frank, but what I and the children did. People recognized the children and remembered them. If they got into any mischief, you can bet your bottom dollar somebody remembered that they were the ones who did it. If there was a crowd, one of them was "that Broyles boy" or "the Broyles girl." This type of thing. But, on the other hand, we've always felt that the benefits of Frank being a coach were so much greater than the unpleasant parts that we didn't mind putting up with a little unpleasantness to have all the good things. We got to travel, meet a lot of interesting people, and do a lot of interesting things that we probably wouldn't have done otherwise.

Many men are gone from home much of the time. One of Frank's brothers had a job that required him to leave the house on Monday morning and come back Friday afternoon, three weeks out of four. Frank was gone all the time. It's a 10-month, 12-hour-a-day job to be a head coach, and almost that much to be an assistant. It's all in the attitude of the wife. If the wife is not resentful of the husband's job, then the children will not be resentful of the father's job.

We thought the time Frank spent at home was really good, and that's better than being at home all the time and being unpleasant. When Daddy came home for dinner, it was a celebration. It might not be but one night a week, but it was a party: Daddy's coming home for dinner! I would guess that almost every promising coach who didn't make it, who switched to another job, probably didn't make it because of his wife. I think that would be generally true of a man in any profession that required him to be away from home a great deal of the time. Some women have different feelings about it, but I always believed a man should be interested in his job, and he ought to get up every morning not being able to wait to go to work. The most horrible thing in the world, I think, would be a man having a job that he dreaded going to in the morning. I worked and I didn't like it, and I would hate to think my husband had to work like that. I was delighted that Frank was always eager about his job.

Frank usually ate at home only on Thursday night during football seasons. Sometimes Wednesday night also. The kids loved for Daddy to be at home; he was always affectionate and involved with them. The support a football wife gives a husband is mainly taking care of the house and children so he doesn't have to worry about what's going on at home.

The wives are so important to a staff. We were on one staff where the wives' outlook was very strange. One didn't even go to the ball games. Another was overly interested and ambitious. Another,

The Broyles children, waiting for their father's induction into the Arkansas Hall of Fame, descend upon the hors d'oeuvres.

though not a gossip, was a talker who spread discontent. The staff was so disrupted that there was never any compatibility between the coaches, and coaches have to work together like a family. They all have ideas. You know, there are 10 ways that every player can move on every play, and eventually you have to narrow it down. They have to be able to throw out their ideas and talk, and then have somebody say, "We're gonna do it this way," and that's the way everybody does it. They can't be worried about one having his say more than the other, and that type of thing. This is where wives can cause trouble because they'll say, "Well, dear, it doesn't seem to me that you get to make decisions like John does." And John's wife is at home saying, "Well, I don't understand why Bill gets all this attention, gets quoted in the papers so much. And I don't like Bill's wife. If we go out, we're going with Joe and his wife." If you are on a staff, everybody has to work together. For years, Frank interviewed wives when he was hiring assistants.

The kids have all been Frank's biggest fans, although they were not rabid or fanatical about it like some people. They were just terribly interested in the Razorbacks and supportive. In the stands at Texas A&M one year, Hank challenged a man who was tearing up his daddy, and Frank told you about Betsy's message in the Cotton Bowl. The nicest part of coaching is to be friends with everybody later on. Like we were at the Sugar Bowl and had a wonderful visit with Archie Manning. He was our big rival once when we played Ole Miss, and Frank has great admiration for his ability. Archie has been complimentary to Frank also, and so now we're friends. Among our former players, we're probably closer to quarterbacks because that was always Frank's field. But we follow all of them and are just as proud when something good happens for them in their job or profession as we were when they played.

All of my life has been spent with athletics. I played when I was young, and I'm a real fan now. I love football, basketball, baseball, and all the others. I have enjoyed everything tremendously.

18
HELP FROM ALL DIRECTIONS

Until I came to Arkansas, I'd never played golf to speak of. Bobby Dodd was a great gamesman. He'd tried everything, won at everything. He often said that the most difficult thing to do in athletics was to make a three-foot putt on the 18th hole, with everything riding.

Dodd did not play much golf, though, when he was Tech's head coach in my time on the staff there. His advice to us was that a coach could not afford to be seen on a golf course. He would be highly visible to powerful people who would later claim that he ought to have been working when he was playing golf. Dodd recommended that we go fishing or play tennis.

During my coaching days at Tech, the only sport I played was tennis, usually as Dodd's doubles partner when he'd force me to come out of the film room. He was a fine doubles player and a state champion with Bitsy Grant at one time.

When I reached Arkansas, I found that the head coach was more or less expected to be an outdoorsman. Many of the leading Razorback supporters loved to fish and hunt. John Barnhill had moved from Tennessee to Arkansas as a result of the urging of fellow deer hunters when he was at a camp near Blytheville in December of 1945.

One of our leading supporters was Rolfe Eldridge, who had a houseboat on the river near his home at Augusta. My first Arkansas summer, in 1958, I found I was supposed to spend a night or two on the boat for some fishing and a barbeque. I brought a book with me (maybe it was Dave Nelson's primer on the winged-T) and spent the night reading it. Anyway, the word got around. I just didn't shoot a gun, so hunting was out. I didn't have the patience for fishing. The worst thing was trout fishing below the big dams. The water was clear and you could see those big things. If they didn't bite, and often they didn't, I felt so frustrated.

So I gravitated to golf. Some of the people I became acquainted with at Little Rock were avid golfers. It became a natural thing to go to Little Rock for four days during the "speaking" season, play golf in the afternoons, and drive 30 to 100 miles each night for a Razorback Club engagement. That led to me becoming almost an everyday golfer from the end of April (or spring practice) until the day before fall practice opened. I'd work half a day, then go to the golf course. I had enough problems with my golf game, and still do, to blot out everything else for four hours: it was total release. A coach who wakes up at three, four, or five o'clock every morning during the football season needs to escape periodically during the year.

Soon after I came to Arkansas, John Cooper, Sr., began enjoying the first of his great successes in the field of vacation-retirement villages. He would have the entire coaching staff over to Cherokee Village, in the beautiful hills along the Spring River, where he'd built a fine golf course. The Coopers, including Joe Basore and George Billingsley, who had married Cooper daughters, became wonderful friends and supporters. They were great at entertaining. One thing led to another, and we started at Cherokee Village the National Coaches Invitational Golf Tournament. Between myself and Bob Cheyne (then the U of A sports information director and now with Cooper Communities, Inc.) we were able to bring in the nation's leading head coaches and sportswriters, first at Cherokee Village, later to Bella Vista Village near Fayetteville, and finally to Hot Springs Village.

What I didn't like was the pressure put on me. Usually I had an agreement that my scores or games wouldn't be published. No special reason, except that golf was my recreation, and I just couldn't see that it concerned anyone. Darrell Royal and I always had the same understanding—we never told who won between us. In the National Coaches tournament, we all had to tee it up for the record. The good thing is that the championship was passed around, and everybody had fun. The bad thing was that I didn't win it as often as I was expected to.

The Coopers made a lot of people happy and gave Arkansas a good name with a lot of prominent visitors. The Coopers had carried the entire economic load, and in time they decided to give it up. The tournament is now held at Dallas. Dr. Pepper, Braniff, the Dallas Cowboys, and other businesses and organizations now share the expense once borne by the Coopers alone. I think the Coopers did it better, but maybe I'm prejudiced.

There was a time, I've heard, when the Arkansas coaching job was subject to political interference. Barnie and his supporters changed that long before I came. I was fortunate in that none of the Arkansas governors in my coaching time wanted to meddle with the football program in any way. All they wanted to do was to help when they could. Orval Faubaus, Winthrop Rockefeller, Dale Bumpers, and David Pryor were alike in that one respect.

The late Dallas P. "Pete" Raney, head of a Little Rock investment firm, was on the Board of Trustees when I was hired. He completed 20 years of service in 1968. In effect, he was the Athletic Committee; the Board invariably went along with his ideas. We were limited in means, but Pete always admired the best in everything. He wanted us to be the best that we could be; he wanted our program to move along. He understood that it started with recruiting, and he knew how important facilities were to recruiting.

Pete was a private man. Actually, I saw little of him and seldom heard from him. It was a pleasure when he did call. Usually he would call other friends of mine at the end of a season, asking what was on my mind, what we needed—what he could do for me. In the same indirect way, the word would get back to him. Usually, Pete sounded out his good friend on our staff, George Cole, or Alan Berry, manager of War Memorial Stadium and coordinator of the Razorback Clubs, or *Gazette* sports editor Orville Henry. Pete felt more comfortable operating that way. And it worked. Pete handled things and got them done with a minimum of fuss.

There was one thing Pete would not let us do for the longest time. He said no to the recruiting of black athletes. Pete was not alone in this thought. His feelings probably reflected those of the Board of his time, the legislature of his time, as well as those of many of the fans. As I pointed out in the chapter on recruiting, there were no black athletes in any of the predominantly white schools in our conference or region during this period. Pete's views first affected

Believe it or not the Razorback on the podium was Governor David Pryor.

Glen Rose and his Arkansas basketball program in 1959. Glen had just come off a co-championship season in '58, and he had a chance to enroll a great basketball player from North Little Rock, Eddie Miles, who went on to Seattle University and the Detroit Pistons. What might have happened if the situation had been otherwise is wistful thinking. What dominated was the political reality and social climate of the times.

Then Pete changed. SMU did not beat us in the three years the Mustangs suited up Southwest Conference trail-blazer Jerry Levias, but Pete, who had been a fine athlete at Hendrix College, was wise enough to read the future. He told us to proceed with the recruitment of black athletes.

There has always been talk about lifetime contracts. Pete Raney, toward the end of his service on the Board, drew up for me the first lifetime contract that I knew about. I conceivably could have coached until I was 67. Pete told me after our 10-1 season in '68 that I

needed a better contract. He pointed out that he wouldn't always be
on the Board, that Dr. David Mullins wouldn't always be president,
and sooner or later I could be placed in a position of dealing with
different people who weren't familiar with the past. The Board
voted to give me tenure, and a contract providing that when the next
vacancy in the athletic director's position occurred (which would be
when George Cole retired in '73) I would have the choice of serving
as both athletic director and head football coach, or as athletic director alone, until I reached retirement age. It provided that I would
be hired for five years, with a one-year extension, and an increase in
salary coming automatically each January 1. As I said, I know of no
other such contract in the profession. My job took on a much different perspective.

If Pete and I seldom had any personal contact, the reverse was
true with Jackson T. "Jack" Stephens. Jack and I are of the same age.
He cultivated my interest in golf, and introduced me to the Augusta
National Golf Club, which subsequently invited me to become a
member. Needless to say, I accepted. Jack is not really a rabid football
fan. He goes to all our Little Rock games and a few others, and he
roots for the Razorbacks (and anything else about the state and the
University), but regardless of his casual interest in football Jack and I
became close friends almost immediately. It was Jack who set up the
packaging of my television show, which was a great recruiting and
public relations tool, as well as a source of outside income.

When I came to Arkansas, the concept of the coach's weekly TV
show was in its infancy all over the country. Channel Four, the NBC
affiliate at Little Rock, wanted me to do just an improvised show each
week—a few highlights, an interview or two, and maybe a little bit
about the huddle, the fair catch, or pass interference or something
like that. I suggested to Channel Four people that they look at Bobby
Dodd's show, which was at that time the most popular TV in Georgia.
It was very simple to do, and I felt it would have a much bigger
impact. They checked with the Atlanta station that handled the
Dodd show, and when they called me back they were enthusiastic
about copying the Dodd format. When we started in 1958, I made
$300 a show. I talked with Bud Campbell about the previous day's
game while we showed the film, and I explained inside factors that
caused us to win or lose, a very basic and very successful format,
which became standard on most coaches' shows. We rocked along

"Jack Stephens and I after the Razorbacks won their 22nd in a row in 1965."

until 1962 when the Arkansas-Louisiana Gas Company pulled out as a sponsor because my show was going to be sponsored by an electric company in the Shreveport market. I had nothing to do with that; Channel Four was selling my show where it could. Jack's brother, W. R. "Witt" Stephens, headed Arkla-Gas at that time, and was also a good friend of mine, and I called Jack to tell him I regretted the way things had worked out.

"Hey," Jack said. "That's the greatest thing in the world. They don't know what they're missing. Let me be responsible for getting the sponsors together for your show."

"Jack, I didn't call you for that," I said. "I just wanted to tell you I was sorry."

"It's the greatest thing in the world," he repeated. He came up with a plan for 10 sponsors, one for each game, then eventually the number grew to 20. Each adjustment meant a considerable increase in money for me, which the Broyles family was definitely able to use. After we beat Texas in 1965, toward the latter part of the 22-game winning streak, Jack and Pete Raney flew to Fayetteville. "Frank," Jack said, "we just don't think it's fair to keep all these people who want to sponsor your show. You've got 10 sponsors but so many more want in that the 10 sponsors want to let other people get in the act. We want to increase it to 20."

I didn't feel it was fair to the original 10, but Jack and Pete kept trying to persuade me. I finally said I would agree if all 10 current sponsors agreed. Jack called me from the meeting. "We took a vote and you lost unanimously," he said. "We're going to 20 sponsors." Of course, I didn't think for a minute that the 20 sponsors came from anything other than the salesmanship of Jack and some others, but they made it possible for the show to be worth a lot more to me personally, and I was grateful.

By this time, we had moved the show to Channel Seven, the ABC affiliate. We switched in 1966. NBC had the American Football League games, and Channel Four could no longer provide the Sunday afternoon time slot that we considered essential. Mostly, though, we moved because Bud Campbell had moved from Channel Four to Channel Seven. I'd always done the show with Bud, who was the most perfect man to work with that I'd ever known. He had no ego. For TV people, that's a little bit unusual because some of them get entranced with the sound of their own voice and they get spoiled to the limelight and everything, but not Bud. He was retiring and I think really a little bit shy off-camera, and you could tell he was embarrassed when somebody thought he'd done a good job. We did about 170 shows together before Bud was killed in an auto accident in 1974, and not one time was I ever agitated by anything that he asked me. We didn't rehearse it; there was no reason. He was a great professional and we were so fortunate to have him in Arkansas. He worked harder than any other four people—he did everything. He worked all the time, the same hours as football coaches.

Here's something that, over the years, has caused a lot of people to wag heads: on any given visit to Little Rock, I might be having lunch in the Board room of Stephens, Inc., one of the largest investment houses in the nation, and then I might walk over to the Tower Building and chat with R. A. "Brick" Lile. Or vice versa. Jack Stephens was one of the chief backers of Orval Faubus, or actually most any Democratic officeholder. Brick was a Republican and a close associate of Winthrop Rockefeller, who followed Faubus as governor. Whether it was politics or business, Brick and Jack didn't mix. I consider each a dear friend, but in different ways, since they are different, and I have been in business ventures with each. Of course, I've always preached that everyone in Arkansas, whatever his persuasion or background, should be for the Razorbacks. I saw nothing amiss with the fact that each was for the team and the head coach, and I was for each of them.

Neither escaped a knock or two in going to bat for me in time of controversy. I regret that, but I'm grateful that they were willing to be counted.

The late W. E. "Bill" Darby was a real benefactor, especially in the early years. Bill had a way of saying, with great emphasis: "I L-U-V the Razorbacks!" and he responded to almost any need we would express. When we won a championship our second year and went on to beat Georgia Tech in the Gator Bowl, Bill and another Little Rock friend and supporter, Jack Pickens, turned the Gator Bowl trip into a 17-day junket. I needed a plane for recruiting and speaking; the Razorback Clubs had grown to 23 or 24 in the state. We had started with three or four, and I had to "do" each one of them each year. One day, I told Barnie and George Cole: "We're up to 23 Razorback Clubs. I can't handle all them, still recruit, coach, and see my family." So we cut it down; I'd do half of them each year, the others the next. Coming back from the Sugar Bowl game after the '62 season, Bill Darby said, "What do you need?" Well, he'd already given us money for a dining hall when we needed a fine training table adjacent to our athletic dorm. Bill knew his athletes. He insisted that it should be built so that the room could be converted to a study hall at night and that there be smaller rooms nearby for tutoring sessions. "Mr. Darby," I said. "You've done enough, but we need an airplane. If we're going to be competitive in recruiting and everything, we've got to have one." He said, "Well, you go buy one and I'll get the money." He, Brick, and Jack each contributed a substantial amount.

Lou Holtz told me not long ago of a visit he'd had with Bear Bryant. He'd asked Bear what was the first, most important thing to do in beginning a new coaching assignment. Bear told him to find "two strong men" he could depend on to get some things done, because there would be things the head coach could not get done without help. When Lou told me that, I realized how lucky I'd been at Arkansas. I had not two, but many.

I'm sure that Bear wound up with far more than "two strong men" behind him at Alabama, as I did. His reference was probably just for starters.

19
PRESS DIPLOMACY

Somebody said once that half the football coaches regard the media as a necessary evil, and the other half look on it as an unnecessary evil. I suppose that was meant to convey that very few coaches, deep down, really enjoy give-and-take sessions with the press. I never thought of it as an adversary relationship. I made up my mind very early that I would be as informative and cooperative with reporters as possible, and then not worry about anything they wrote, good or bad. I found dealing with the press stimulating and enjoyable (most of the time).

I've always been very proud of the assessment of me written by Dan Jenkins before Dan gained national recognition as an outstanding reporter *(Sports Illustrated)* and author *(Semi-tough):*

Frank Broyles is the best thing that has happened to newspapermen since budget accounts. His enthusiasm, wit, and intellect make him more fun to be around than a White River yellow cat.

This is the freshest impression of a Southwest Conference hitch-hiker who has just returned from a 2,000-mile bus ride (the pre-season press tour) to find out (a) who is going to beat whom in 1962 (b) what people do in Lubbock after nine o'clock at night and (c) Waco's future schedule for tornadoes.

Up at Arkansas, Broyles held two interviews, one of them impromptu, which should have been taped and sent to all college coaches so they could learn something about public relations.

Broyles has that enviable quality of remembering names, of making everyone feel welcome, relaxed, and comfortable. He gives freely of his own mind in a seemingly natural, uncautious, and trusting way. The Razorbacks' coach has a wonderful humor, an appreciation for the original anecdote, and a keen mind for the obscure dimensions of his craft.

He is obviously a master salesman and a great coach or he would not have enjoyed three straight championships already. Still, he has a way of winning over strangers and making them pull for him to win more.

He must read all of the papers around the conference because he knows where everyone has been and what they've been doing. He loves to talk—and listen. And he is not confined to the subject of football, which is so true of most coaches.

Most of the 16 writers on the tour agreed that if they were involved with hiring a coach anywhere in the country—and could have any man they wanted—they would take Frank Broyles.

"He'll always give you something good to write," is the way most of us describe him. And you'll have to pardon us for being selfish in the matter."

The Razorbacks had a generous, supportive press in Arkansas and even-handed treatment in Texas, by and large. Of course, if you live in Arkansas (or maybe anywhere in this region) you know that I was closer to Orville Henry, sports editor of the *Arkansas Gazette,* than any other writer. Usually a coach and a writer can enjoy no more than a good, compatible working relationship, but Orville and I became personal friends. We are about the same age, we had the same size family (four boys) when we first met, and we hit it off immediately. I had great faith in Orville, and I marveled at his insight into the thinking of our football team, the strength of our team, and what our problems were. I could always confide in him. Often, as we talked on Sundays and Mondays about the game just over and the game coming up, he gave me ideas that helped me prepare my team. He understood game strategy and players' psychology and fans' psychology in a way that was almost unique for a sportswriter. Over the years, Orville wrote some things that I thought we could have been better off without, but I never tried to tell him how to write and he never tried to tell me how to coach.

You talk about foresight. Here is Orville's description of the scene at Big Shootout I with Texas on December 6, 1969:

"You're there. President Nixon is there. Mickey Herskowitz, maybe even Red Smith is there. Chris Schenkel and Bud Wilkinson and a 67-man ABC-TV crew are there. Hoss Cartwright is there. The landscape is wintry rather than autumnal but Razorback

Stadium glows with color, red and burnt orange on all sides of the fluorescent-green AstroTurf, flags flying, balloons ascending. The time is at hand for the most ballyhooed kick-off in Southwest Conference history. Arkansas and Texas, 9-0 on each side of the field, are playing for the national collegiate football championship.

That's 100 per cent correct in all essential details. I can't recall if Hoss Cartwright made it, but Billy Graham did. Orville didn't write this on December 6, though. It had appeared in the *Gazette* back in August.

Few people would recall it now, but Jim Mooty withdrew from football in 1959 and planned to pass up his senior year because he was worried about headaches. He wasn't out for spring practice; he wasn't listed on the pre-season roster. Now, I think everybody in Arkansas and Texas had it in the back of their minds that Mooty would come back and play, but he was officially out and we had to make other plans. We looked at a lot of halfbacks that spring—Lance Alworth, Billy Kyser, Bruce Fullerton, Jarrell and Darrell Williams, Harold Horton—in a search to replace our meal ticket at left halfback. Alworth was coming up to his sophomore year but so much was expected of him by the fans and the press that I went overboard, as young coaches will, trying to keep the heat off. I declined to speculate on who might win the No. 1 job at left half in September. One Saturday during the spring Lance had a sensational scrimmage. He did everything; he looked like a million dollars. Orville was there and he wrote the next day that Lance was certain to start at left half. Only one thing would prevent it, he said: An All-American would have to beat him out. I winced a little, because that just didn't fit with my no-pressure campaign. Mooty came back. He played left halfback and made All-American. Lance started at right half. When the season ended, I told Orville: "Well, you were right. It took an All-American to beat him out."

Several weeks before I retired in 1976, I informed a few close friends of my decision because I knew they'd be hurt if they learned of it second-hand. That included Orville. He "broke" the story a couple of days before our final game against Texas. He wanted the story to have full attention in Arkansas before it became obvious that Darrell was retiring also. I didn't tell him to break it; I informed him in confidence and counted on his good judgement. I think he made the right decision.

Aside from the retirement decision, which I regarded as a personal matter, I did no more to keep Orville informed than I did any other writer. A few, maybe looking for a crutch, griped that he had some special pipeline. He did; it was called a telephone. He picked it up and used it. He called and asked, and I told him. He worked hard at staying on top of his job. When any writer called and asked questions, I laid out the facts as I understood them. I always tried to make sure they all got a story.

About 1970, an *Arkansas Democrat* sports columnist, Fred Morrow, launched a "Who Says Frank Broyles is Any Good?" school of journalism and constantly baited Razorback fans with a needling, bantering mix of innuendo and rumor. People assumed Morrow and I were involved in some personal vendetta. I didn't even know him. We had maybe two conversations in the six years he wrote for the *Democrat*. Once, I remember, he called and asked about the youngster who donned a red hog mascot outfit and served as the "dancing Razorback." I don't recall that he ever asked anything pertaining directly to the football team. He picked up his football information elsewhere. I was willing to talk to him at any time and cooperate with him in any way, but apparently he figured he was doing all right without any help from me. I'd enjoyed a very good relationship with his predecessor, Jack Keady.

From the beginning, Barbara and I always had a little gathering for our coaches and their wives after a game at Fayetteville. As time went along, I started inviting this or that writer to come for dinner, because I knew how tough it was for them to get into a restaurant. A reporter generally has one to three hours' work in the press box after a football game, and it's tough to walk out at 7 p.m. and find a place to eat when 40,000 people have a head start on you. So it just evolved that one or two, or seven or eight, or 10 or 12 of our newspaper friends would join us for dinner. At that stage of the evening, win or lose, I usually felt like talking and unwinding. The aftermath of a game didn't catch up with me until about nine o'clock, and that's about the time the group usually broke up.

The worst time for a writer to try to talk to a coach is in the dressing room immediately after the game. At that point, you don't feel like venturing beyond a few general statements, but writers have deadlines and can't wait for you to pick the film apart. Other than a running back or a passer or a receiver, you hesitate to discuss individual players. The linebacker who sacked the quarterback three times (and caught everybody's eye) may have had a bad day overall. The offensive lineman that nobody mentioned may have actually out-executed everybody on the field.

I never publicly disavowed a quote attributed to me, no matter how wrong or out of context it might be. I never called a writer and complained about a story. If he was wrong, he lived with it; if he was correct, he lived with it. I found that most writers I dealt with were fair and responsible men who wanted to do the best job they could. If they made a mistake, they'd find it out themselves and learn from it. The exceptions were simply not worth worrying about.

20
A TIME TO RETIRE

Colonel Earl "Red" Blaik, who had those powerhouse teams at Army through the 1940s and '50s, was a coach I greatly admired from a distance. I never had a chance to know him well, but I placed him on a plateau with a very few other coaches as a leader of my profession. Some of Blaik's disciples, his former assistants, told me he often lectured them about getting out of coaching by the time they were 45. That stuck in my mind for some reason, and became one of my goals. I missed it by about six years, but you might be surprised how close I came to hitting it right on the nose.

I was tempted to retire after the 1970 season. If we had beaten Texas in '70, in the Big Shootout rematch at Austin, I might have retired then. It was very much on my mind, but nobody knew that except Barbara. She kept telling me I wasn't ready. "You just think you are," she said. We talked about my retiring all through the early '70s, talked about choosing the proper time.

Then, all of a sudden, our program went down. We were so far behind in facilities by 1972 that our recruiting had suffered tremendously. We were recruiting negatively. We would bring a prospect to our campus and say, for example, "Well, you don't have to have a nice weight room. Just so you've got weights. And we're out here in the 'half-house,' you know, and it's cold, but you've got an old gas heater in there. And you don't have to have big fancy dressing rooms or indoor workout areas or anything like that. Education is the most important thing."

This was the way we had to recruit at that time. Really.

I talked to President David Mullins in 1972 and received his permission to go before the Board of Trustees. I told them we needed to upgrade our facilities or we needed to drop out of the Southwest Conference, one or the other. "It's to that point," I said. "I don't want to sound like a prophet of doom, but unless we can make improvements, we can never again be competitive in the Southwest Conference." I suggested that we start a new contribution program, tied to the ticket sales and based on priority, and commit the money to improve our facilities. "The school can't give us any money; that's obvious," I said. "The state can't give us any. The only way we can raise money is through gifts."

The Board agreed and authorized us to go ahead with our new scholarship plan. In 1973 we had the money coming in and I had to make a decision whether to upgrade football or basketball. We didn't have enough money to do both. I decided we'd better do everything we could to get football going again. If we turned the football program around, we could then upgrade basketball and the other sports. So we built an incredible athletic plant, the North End Zone Facility. When we started showing recruiting prospects the forms after the concrete had been poured, and showing them pictures of what the finished product would be, our recruiting picked up considerably. It was a touch of sweet irony that the first year we were in the new building, 1975, we tied for the Conference championship and made our first trip to the Cotton Bowl in 10 years.

There is nothing in America to equal the North End Zone Facility. I think it is the finest building of its kind, and my opinion is shared by almost all athletic directors and coaches who have seen it. People from colleges all over the country came to look it over and told us that, with costs mounting as they are, it can never be duplicated. We'll have the only one. There will never be another multipurpose athletic plant like it—certainly not for the same money, or any sum close to it.

I really wanted to follow Colonel Blaik's advice in 1970, but Barbara talked me out of it. Then, from '72 until '75, we knew I couldn't retire until the program was restored. For one thing, we couldn't hire the kind of replacement we'd want with everything at such a low ebb. Who'd want to step into that situation? This was the practical consideration, but there was another. My pride demanded that we get things rolling again before I quit.

Some people told us that the priority plan would never stand up;

that it would be too controversial and devisive. We were not dealing from a position of strength. Our teams were going 6-5, 5-5-1, 6-4-1, rather than the 9-2 or 10-1 that our fans had come to expect in the '60s. Anytime you lose or anytime you don't win big, you must expect criticism. When Bill Pace was the head coach at Vanderbilt, he was winding up an unsuccessful year when he told me, "Frank, I haven't had a single bad call or a bad letter from anybody." I told him that he had the wrong job. "The worst thing is if they don't care," I said. "When you don't win, you expect them to be unhappy."

Dr. Raymond Miller, the first black member of our Board of Trustees, proved to be a tower of strength in those difficult times, both with the priority plan and the recruitment of black athletes. He turned it around for us in the black community.

We started the 1973 season with only two established senior football players, linebacker Danny Rhodes and tailback Dickey Morton. I still marvel at Dickey Morton. He was a 180-pounder who had to run where the traffic was heavy all the time, but he never missed a game in three years while he set conference records for carries (595) and yardage (3,317). In his senior year, we had a thin and inexperienced team and couldn't get anything established, but Dickey gained 1298 yards. We lettered 10 freshmen that year, which helped later on. We were a good team in spots in '74 and in '75, we hit the top again with a 10-2 season climaxed by that great upset of Texas A&M on national television.

Why didn't I quit after the '75 season and the Cotton Bowl win over Georgia? Well, things were going so good that I wasn't sure I wanted to quit. It just didn't seem to be the right time. Then the recruiting that year got awfully tough, and in the middle of the '76 season, I told Al Witte, our faculty representative, that I was going to retire at the end of the season, regardless.

At the time, I thought we'd win it again. We had just beaten Houston (which wound up in the Cotton Bowl), and we looked to be the best team in the league at that time. But then our sophomore quarterback, Ron Calcagni, got hurt and everything changed. We didn't have any offense after that, and our defensive team finally lost its morale when it saw we couldn't score. We stood 5-1 in midseason and we finished 5-5-1. But that had no bearing on my decision, which had been made and was irreversible.

I've told you that Darrell and I confided our retirement decisions to each other during the season. I didn't think he'd live up to his, and he told me later he didn't think I'd live up to mine.

Three weeks before the last game, I gave Dr. Charles Bishop, our president, a letter of resignation. I immediately had Lou Holtz in mind as my successor. I had known Lou from the time that I was on the Board of the Coaches Association and Lou served as secretary. He was then coaching at William and Mary. I got to know him better when he came to a couple of our coaches' golf tournaments. I also knew him through Bo Rein, the offensive coach who came to us from Lou's staff at North Carolina State (and who replaced him there when Lou went to the New York Jets). I really admired Lou's ability to bring back a program, to be the underdog and win. In the summer of '76, I'd called him about a tryout for one of our players, Roland Fuchs, and Lou told me he felt like a fish out of water in pro football. "Keep it confidential," he said. "but I may be looking for a college job."

After I told Al Witte I was going to retire, I thought I'd better call Lou to be sure he didn't line up with somebody else in case he left the Jets. "I know where a great job's gonna be," I said. "It'll be one of the top jobs in America. I hope you're interested."

Lou laughed. "Arkansas?" he asked. I said yes, and he said, "Well good." We left it at that for the time being. I didn't talk to him again until after my retirement story broke. I had alerted him, and neither of us was in a position to go beyond that. I felt that the school would want me to select the new coach, but I had no confirmation of it until I turned in my letter. Dr. Bishop told me he wanted me to pick a successor for him to take to the Board.

Lou planned to announce his resignation from the Jets after the season was over, and come down for a visit. He had two or three other job offers. The Jets told him they wanted him to stay, but they'd give him a release from his contract with no problem. An hour before the scheduled press conference, they asked him not to resign. He called me, and I told him he was vacillating like a high school quarterback. I got Darrell and Doug Dickey and some of my other coaching friends to call him. Lou was torn between his desire to get back to college coaching and the pleas of the Jets management. His situation required thought rather than emotion. He called me back the next morning. He'd thought it out and talked with his wife, and he was resigning. He would be interested in interviewing for the Arkansas job.

He resigned, flew on into Fayetteville that weekend, and accepted the job. I told everybody he'd take the state by storm, and I wasn't talking about magic tricks and one-liners. Lou's first season, 11-1, was capped by one of the great victories in Arkansas history—that 31-6 Orange Bowl conquest of an Oklahoma team that everybody except the Razorbacks considered unbeatable.

Lou realized Arkansas was a quality opportunity, but I don't think he was prepared for the impact the Razorbacks have on the state. There's no way anybody can be prepared for that until they see and feel it first-hand. In his situation at North Carolina State, they had four or five major schools practically on each other's doorstep.

The hiring of Eddie Sutton was a stroke of pure luck. I had called some of my friends in the basketball profession, trying to get the best possible coach I could secure. At the time, I didn't think we could attract a successful head basketball coach to Arkansas. I was more or less looking for a top assistant in a winning program. Eddie's name cropped up everywhere I went, but I didn't even think it was worth a call. Eddie's Creighton University team was eliminated from the NCAA regional at Tulsa, and *Tulsa World* sports editor Bill Connors alerted me to the fact that Eddie would be interested. "You've got to be kidding," I said, or at least that's what I thought. I interviewed Eddie and Patsy, and then he went on to watch the NCAA finals at Greensboro. Eddie couldn't make up his mind, so I flew to Greensboro and we talked until he agreed to take the job.

Hiring Eddie, who was obviously one of the brightest young coaches in the country, was our first step in removing the second-class stigma from basketball. Football had first priority and everybody knew it—the fooball coaches knew it, the basketball coaches knew it, the football players knew it, the basketball players knew it, the students knew it, the fans knew it. For a long time, we didn't have money to do more than support the football program. When we set up the new contribution plan in 1972, however, we pledged that money to building facilities for all sports. Eddie, of course, would not have come if we hadn't made a commitment to renovate old Barnhill Fieldhouse into Barnhill Arena, and do our best to build the strongest basketball program possible.

Several people whose opinions I highly respected advised me against the basketball decision. When I asked Lon Ferrell to jog my memory on several matters during the preparation of this book, Lon reminded me he had argued that the state and the Fayetteville area didn't have the population to support a national basketball power along with football. Of course, the basketball program moved along much faster than any of us had dared hope in the beginning.

Sutton was hired in the spring of 1974. His teams were competitive instantly, and in their third year, they swept the Southwest Conference round robin. In their fourth, they reached the NCAA Final Four. In their fifth, supposedly a rebuilding year, they tied for their third straight conference championship and qualified for the NCAA Regional again, and in the space of those three hectic, wonderful years, our fans became rabid about basketball. Before the turnaround, our top basketball income for one season was about $30,000. Last year, the figure was more like $900,000. Basketball is self-sustaining now, to say the very least. More people saw our basketball team play "live" in 1978-79 than ever saw our football team, thanks to 18 televised regular season games, plus the NCAA tournament.

Our baseball team dramatized the resurgence of our spring sports by coming within a whisker of winning the College World Series in June of '79. We knew that to get competitive in baseball, we had to join the Southwest Conference race. That had never been feasible because of our facilities, the weather, etc., but as soon as we could get an AstroTurf baseball field, we joined the conference and the whole picture changed.

Let me brag a little. In the last three years, our total athletic program reached parity with the best in the nation regardless of location, population, or whatever. The future is brighter still.

I wanted the Arkansas job originally, because of the opportunity to work for John Barnhill, and because of the obvious advantages of one state unified behind one University. When Barnie called me at Columbia, Missouri, to offer me the job, I immediately looked at an Atlas to try to learn something about the state. (Geography was never one of my strong points, as my sixth-grade teacher could attest.) I saw that Fayetteville was way up in the Northwest corner. I remembered that during my time at Baylor, Southwest Conference people always complained about that long haul into the mountains. "At least, I know they've got mountains there," I thought.

While I was coaching, I never went to the Hall of Fame dinners or the big Touchdown Club banquets around the country. Maybe I should have gone, maybe it would have helped Arkansas, but it was

"The happiest Athletic Director in the U.S.A."

in recruiting season, and I didn't think I could spare the time. Darrell and some of my other friends went, and they told me they thought it hurt their recruiting.

If I had it all to do over again, I would change many things. At least, I believe I would—that's the advantage of hindsight. I would try to be tougher because many people have told me, in one way or another, that that was one of my weaknesses. I don't know if I could manage it or not, because that's not my nature and you make a mistake to try to coach like anybody but yourself.

I wanted the University of Arkansas to be above reproach in every respect. Bobby Dodd had always lived by the rules, and from the beginning of my career, I was determined that no hint of dishonesty would ever be associated with my program. There would be no illegal short-cuts. If we had to break the rules to win, then we'd just lose. We wouldn't step over the line.

I didn't know how many championships I'd win and I didn't know what they would say about me as a tactician on the field, but I intended that when it was all over, they'd have to look back and say,

"Well, Broyles ran an honest, clean, above-board program." Anything we gained, we would gain honestly. It would have killed me if my school had ever been found guilty of recruiting violations.

Imagine my horror when I learned in 1966 that we were under investigation by the NCAA for arranging transportation for two Lawton, Oklahoma, prospects to our Cotton Bowl game against LSU. We didn't even know they were there until Jim Mackenzie spotted them. One was Jerry Dossey, who became a fine player for us, and the other was a fullback named Baldwin who went to Oklahoma. We were recruiting them heavily, as were many other schools. Oklahoma State turned us in.

As I recall the sequence of circumstance pieced together by our attorney, E. J. Ball, it went like this: Gene Goff, a Fayetteville businessman, had four Cotton Bowl tickets he found he would be unable to use. At Tulsa, he ran into Bob Griffin, an outstanding U of A lineman of 1949-51, one of Barnie's last and best recruits. Goff offered Griffin the tickets. Bob said he couldn't go, but he'd send them to a U of A teammate, Jim Rinehart from this hometown of Fredrick, Oklahoma. Rinehart hadn't seen a U of A game in about 10 or 15 years. He lived at Lawton then. Rinehart knew Baldwin well and took an interest in helping him because the boy was fatherless. He offered one of the tickets to Baldwin and suggested he take another and bring along a friend. The friend turned out to be the other top prospect, Dossey.

We obtained affadavits, checked everything, and could find no involvement by any of our people. Neither could the NCAA, but the investigators wouldn't believe us because of the amazing coincidence. As one man on the committee phrased it, "Can you explain how an alumnus, who hadn't been to an Arkansas game in years, suddenly appears at a game with two football players?"

Nobody could except George Cole. George sat in there and listened and listened. Finally, he spoke up. "I'll tell you why. Both of 'em came from Fredrick."

I don't know how or why, but that cleared us.

The Southwest Conference also investigated us for a technicality involving procedure, not money. Two Pine Bluff prospects, Jim Barnes and Gordon Norwood, made a basketball trip with their high school team to Fort Smith. Since they were that close, we invited them to come on to Fayetteville for a visit before returning home. We weren't supposed to do that. Under those circumstances, they must return home with their high school team. If they had returned to Pine Bluff and turned around and immediately driven to Fayetteville, that would have been fine. We were ignorant or careless in that instance, and someone filed a complaint with the conference.

At that SWC meeting, Texas and SMU received probation without sanctions in two other incidents under consideration. To our dismay, they then voted to make it three and give Arkansas a slap on the wrist also. One faculty representative from a Texas school stood up in the meeting and said, "This is silly. There's not a thing in the world against them. This is nothing." We agreed.

College athletics, if conducted in the proper atmosphere, and with the proper safeguards and philosophy, can be the greatest life example in the world for the student-athletes, the other students, the coaches, the school, and everyone concerned. What kind of example is set and what ideals are upheld by breaking the rules? The whole process is tarnished. It all becomes pointless, cyncial, and self-defeating.

In the fall of 1977, writers assembled for the first of the Lou Holtz-Fred Akers Arkansas and Texas shootouts asked me what I found hardest about being out of harness with a big game coming up.

"I didn't realize how difficult it was to get to the ball game without a police escort," I said.

Retired coaches had told me they had no trouble with football homesickness except on game day when they'd start thinking, "Well, we'd be eating the pre-game meal right now," or "It's time to tape." I found a wonderful escape from that sort of thing by going to other people's games. One year, ABC-TV used active coaches for "color" commentary. One weekend when our team was idle, they assigned me to the Texas-Texas A&M game, and NCAA officials and some other people spoke favorably to ABC about my work in the game. They gave me a chance to do it again, then they put me in the Gator Bowl, and by the time I retired from coaching, I'd handled four or five games and I was totally fascinated.

Jim Lindsey and I had made some plans for me to do some real estate work for the company in which I was a partner with Jim. I was going to get my real estate agent's license and try to fill the slack time that I didn't have when I was coaching. Something to keep me busy, and not fretting away my time or regretting being away from coaching.

Before I could get started with that, ABC officials called me in February of 1977 and asked if I would like to do some games. I checked with our president, Dr. Bishop, and he said it was okay, so I set my new course as an athletic director and part-time TV announcer. The games have been excellent therapy for me in so many ways, and I worked hard and tried to do a good job. I hope it's been good for Arkansas, and Lou and Eddie both feel it's been very helpful to their programs. Southwest Conference officials and faculty reps have written letters to the effect that it's been good for the conference. Of course, it's a fickle business—more fickle than coaching, even—and you never know if it'll last a year or two, or what. I appreciate the kind comments from viewers and network people and especially from play-by-play professionals like Keith Jackson and Chris Schenkel, and others that I've been fortunate to work with.

When I started my new career as athletic director and broadcaster (or part-time real estate man, or whatever), I pledged I would develop more close friendships and enjoy the fellowship of my friends and my family. These are the most important things in my life. In 30 years of coaching, I was close to the glorious but missed the glory of it all. Your family learns to understand, but, like a lot of other people in my profession or other professions, I became so wrapped up in working toward the goals of my job I tended to overlook what motivated me in the first place.

I believe if I had my coaching career to do all over, I could strike a better balance between family and friends and job—and have just as much success. I'm not sure just how I'd manage that, but I'd like to think I could. However, all 30 years were a labor of love. I'm grateful I was a part of the coaching world. I value the friends I have made and the young men I was fortunate to coach. I hope my life has been of value to them. If so, then I've been lucky.